~~Paris 22222298~~

~~Tunis 272.483~~

South–South Financial Co-operation

South–South Financial Co-operation

Approaches to the Current Crisis—The Jamaica Papers

Edited by

Dragoslav Avramovic

Frances Pinter (Publishers), London

First published in Great Britain in 1983 by
Frances Pinter (Publishers) Limited
5 Dryden Street, London WC2E 9NW

British Library Cataloguing in Publication Data

South-South financial cooperation
1. Underdeveloped areas—Economic policy—Congresses 2. Underdeveloped areas—Economic conditions—Congresses
I. Avramovic, Dragoslav II. Centre for Research on the New International Economic Order
330.9172'4 HC59.7

ISBN 0-86187-337-8

Typeset by Joshua Associates, Oxford
Printed by SRP Ltd., Exeter

CONTENTS

FOREWORD

In May 1981, a high-level meeting of the Group of 77 was held in Caracas and a plan of action was agreed upon which covered both the research and follow-up of the main items appearing in the Declaration on the New International Economic Order. Among these items was the question of finance and a number of meetings and research Papers were suggested to help the G.77 to come to a final decision on the best ways and means of South–South co-operation in the field of finance.

On the question of financial co-operation, Dr Dragoslav Avramovic was assigned the task of organizing an expert group meeting of the Group of 77 in Jamaica in late March 1982. The Papers contained in this book are the edited versions of those submitted to this meeting. One of the most interesting recommendations to come out of the Jamaica meeting was that a technical study on the feasibility of a bank for developing countries should be undertaken. A meeting convened in Manila in the late summer of 1982 of the Group of 77 endorsed this recommendation and decided to go ahead with the study. The work of this study is now being organized and hopefully will be ready for the next meeting of UNCTAD in June 1983 in Yugoslavia.

We have undertaken to publish this work in an effort to present other alternatives to the current financial crisis, which is not only inflicting recession and high unemployment on the industrial world (the North), but also more seriously affecting the developing countries (the South).

The basic idea behind these Papers is that the developing countries should try to utilize their own resources and come up with new institutions and modalities for development and other financing. The most dangerous thing they could do now would be to wait for the industrial countries to solve their own problems and hopefully those of the developing world. If the North is in no mood at present to take the initiative, there is no reason why the South should not do so.

January 1983

Dr Salah Al-Shaikhly, Executive Director
Centre for Research on the NIEO, Oxford

ACKNOWLEDGEMENTS

The Centre for Research on the New International Economic Order is grateful to UNCTAD for giving us permission to use the Jamaica Papers. We very much appreciate the efforts of Dr Dragoslav Avramovic, who not only pioneered this idea but also actively contributed to the main theme appearing in Chapter 1 and helped us in editing the remainder of the book.

Our thanks also go to the authors, who permitted us to publish their Papers and collaborated with us in up-dating and making corrections.

1 FINANCIAL CO-OPERATION AMONG DEVELOPING COUNTRIES: ISSUES AND OPPORTUNITIES

DRAGOSLAV AVRAMOVIC

Introduction

1. This chapter sets out the issues believed to be central to financial co-operation among developing countries and explores in particular the case for the establishment of a bank for developing countries. The chapter is a revised version of the main document which was submitted to the Expert Group meeting of the Group of 77 in Jamaica on 26-31 March 1982, under the title, 'The Jamaica Meeting on Finance: Major Questions'. In addition, it includes the findings of another document submitted in Jamaica, entitled, 'The Caracas Programme on Finance: Substance and Implementation'.

2. The chapter consists of six sections. The first section provides a summary of the decisions on financial co-operation among developing countries reached at the High-Level Conference on Economic Co-operation among Developing Countries held in Caracas, Venezuela, on 13–19 May 1981. The second section focuses on the guiding thoughts in the preparation of the documentation for the Jamaica meeting as to the nature of South-South financial co-operation. The third section contains a brief analysis of the gaps in the international financial structure which may in part be met through such co-operation. The fourth section handles the issue of resource mobilization. The fifth section discusses the institutional issues. The paper ends with a section on the implications of a Third World financial institution for the reconstruction of the international financial and monetary system.

I Caracas decisions on finance

Scope

3. A wide range of subject matter was covered and a detailed negotiating procedure was set out in the Caracas decisions, arranged in eight substantive areas within an impressive conceptual framework:

(i) *Balance of payments support*, with a double decision:
   (a) The feasibility is to be examined of establishing a balance of payments facility contributed by interested developing countries and administered by them (para. 66b);[1] and
   (b) The modalities are to be worked out of a jointly contributed and administered developed–developing country mechanism to alleviate the burden borne by the latter on account of increased prices of imports from developed countries and of imports of petroleum; such a proposal would then be submitted to developed countries (para. 67).

(ii) *Development financing*, presumably lending for specific projects, again with a double decision (para. 79). Concrete measures are to be proposed concerning:
   (a) The entry into force of the Non-Aligned Solidarity Fund, agreed some time back; and
   (b) The establishment of a bank for developing countries as indicated in the Arusha decision of G77. The latter had requested the UNCTAD secretariat to submit a report on the practical feasibility of such a bank taking into account the existing institutions.

(iii) *Joint ventures, other joint projects and direct investment*, with three decisions:
   (a) The following fields are specified: food production, agricultural inputs, fishery equipment including vessels; energy and energy-related equipment; raw materials development, exploiting, processing, marketing, distribution and transhipment; petrochemicals and chemicals; intermediate and capital goods industries, textiles, forest-based industries; and building materials (paras 29, 31b, 32a, 47, 48, 60 and 63);
   (b) Regional and subregional banks are to establish

facilities to undertake equity investments and promote co-financing of equity investments particularly from other developing countries (para. 68), subject, however, to particular circumstances of each institution (para. 69);

(c) Investment incentives, joint venture agreements and other instruments to enhance intra-developing countries' capital flows are to be elaborated (para. 71); and greater awareness of investment opportunities is to be promoted (para. 72).

(iv) *Trade financing*, presumably primarily export financing. Immediate attention is to be given to the setting-up of regional and interregional trade development banks and to the strengthening and broadening of participation of the existing regional ones (presumably *Bladex* in Latin America). Work is to continue on the establishment of the Export Credit Guarantee Facility in UNCTAD (para. 70b).

(v) *Payments arrangements*. Bilateral, subregional and regional schemes should be reinforced, and linkages among them should be devised in order to facilitate interregional payments arrangements (para. 70c).

(vi) *Mutual help schemes* (para. 70). Four steps are singled out:

(a) Increase of deposits in other developing country banks;

(b) Increased purchase of securities issued by developing countries in the international capital market;

(c) Taking fuller advantage of the opportunities to borrow in the capital markets of other developing countries; and

(d) Possibly, assistance by stronger developing countries to the weaker ones to gain access to the international capital market.

(vii) *Financing of commodity stocks*. Two schemes are envisaged:

(a) Acquisition and maintenance of food reserves, including infrastructure requirements (storage, marketing, transportation and port facilities) (para. 30a); and

(b) Consideration is to be given to the study to be prepared by the group of experts of the Non-Aligned countries on the proposal by Madagascar for setting up a stabilization fund (para. 59d).

(viii) *Miscellaneous*. Included are:

(a) Financial investments needed to facilitate the speedy transfer of technology among developing countries (para. 24d);[2]

(b) Financial co-operation in research and development in agriculture (para. 34j) and energy (para. 53b); and

(c) Information flow on development projects undertaken in developing countries is to be organized in order to enable other developing countries to engage effectively in international competitive bidding for execution of these projects (para. 74).

Institutions

4. Two recommendations were made concerning institutional innovation and change:

(i) Establishment of trade development banks (para. 70b, see also above);

(ii) Increasing the capital of existing regional and subregional development banks comprising industrialized and developing countries; increasing developing countries' share in such capital and thus in their participation in decision-making; enlarging the membership of these banks to include all developing countries in the region (presumably reference to Cuba and other similar cases); and the establishment in such banks of facilities to promote direct investment (para. 68, see also above). However, all this is subject to particular circumstances and procedures of each bank (para. 69, see also above).

5. The need and feasibility of possible major innovations, such as the establishment of new balance of payments support facilities and a bank for developing countries, are to be examined by expert groups as shown below.

Negotiating framework

6. A major negotiating machinery has been envisaged to carry out the above programme. No less than seven groups of experts of developing countries are to be established:

(i) The expert group on balance of payments financing facility of developing countries, bank for developing countries, and the entry into force of the Non-Aligned Solidarity Fund;

(ii) The expert group on the joint developed-developing country mechanism to alleviate the burden on the balances of payments of the latter arising from import price increases;

(iii) Technical group of experts to elaborate on investment incentives and other instruments to enhance intra-developing countries' capital flows, including treaties to avoid double taxation;

(iv) Another group consisting of appropriate authorities is to meet to exchange information and elaborate details concerning the needed improvement of the institutional framework of developing countries to ensure greater awareness of investment opportunities;

(v) An expert group should meet to carry out a study on possible arrangements for the preparation of joint projects and other modalities for further developing, exploiting and processing of raw material resources of developing countries;

(vi) A group of experts should be convened to prepare a project on a scheme for acquiring and maintaining food reserves, including the financial arrangements; and

(vii) A technical group of experts is to be set up to study the ways and means for the dissemination of relevant information to assist developing countries in international competitive bidding.

7. For the meetings of two of the above groups, location has been determined: Baghdad for group (ii), and Geneva for group (v). Location for the rest will have to be decided shortly, in view of the timetable (see below).

8. Parallel with the work of the above expert groups of the Group of 77, there will be some activity of the Group of 24 in the implementation of the Caracas decisions. The Group of 24 is called on to continue its work and in particular to give greater attention to monetary and financial aspects within the programme of ECDC (para. 73). The Group of 24, it will be recalled, acts for the developing countries in Bretton Woods

institutions, and particularly in the International Monetary Fund.

Timetable

9. A formidable timetable was set in Caracas. The expert groups on investment incentives, investment opportunities, food reserve stocks financing, joint projects in raw materials, and international competitive bidding ((iii), (iv), (v), (vi) and (vii) above, respectively) were to meet in the third quarter of 1981. The expert groups on balance of payments financing facilities and on development finance ((i) and (ii) above) were to meet in the fourth quarter of 1981. The timetable could not be kept. The expert groups (i) and (ii) met in Jamaica and Baghdad respectively, during March 1982, and the expert group (vi) in Manila in August 1982. Initiative was taken for work on investment opportunities and incentives, but no expert group meeting was held by the end of 1982. With the Baghdad and Jamaica meetings, however, such key policy areas as balance of payments financing facilities and development finance were covered. The result of the Baghdad meeting was to hold off further action on a jointly contributed and administered developed–developing country mechanism to alleviate balance of payments pressures resulting from increased import prices as it was clear that such an action was unlikely under present circumstances. The result of the Jamaica meeting was to embark on a technical study of the feasibility of a bank for developing countries—see Section VI below.

Substantive issues

10. The Caracas programme has several distinguishing features. First it is a remarkably comprehensive programme; it covers almost the whole spectrum of financial relations among developing countries as well as an important segment of their relations with the outside world. Secondly, it is a bold, non-marginalistic programme. The pride of place belongs to the key policy areas: balance of payments support, development lending, direct investment, export financing. Most of these schemes are of world-wide, interregional nature. Thirdly, it is a sophisticated programme, in design and execution. Each component stands on its own feet; and some would involve fine operations in the international capital market. It is not a blueprint of ready-made

solutions, but a detailed programme of work which, taken seriously, may yield lasting results. Finally, it is a programme of collective self-reliance, but it is not a substitute for global financial co-operation. Some parts of it are directly of a global nature, e.g. the mechanism to alleviate the burden of imported inflation is envisaged as a joint developed–developing country effort (it will be recalled that this is the original proposal by Iraq at UNCTAD V); the export financing schemes will cover exports in all directions; increased operations and participation in regional and sub-regional development banks refer to institutions which are joint developed–developing country bodies; and joint ventures and direct investment will frequently involve tripartite participation.

11. An important exception from the comprehensive nature of the Caracas programme is the absence of any provision for broadening, possible liberalization and provision of additional resources to the existing monetary reserve arrangements among central banks of developing countries (reciprocal credit and swap schemes) and possible introduction of new schemes. The examples of such present schemes are the Andean Reserve Fund, Arab Monetary Fund, the ASEAN Swap Arrangement, and the Central American Monetary Council. The reasons for this omission are not clear. It may have been an oversight. With growing balance of payments difficulties experienced by most developing countries and with the curtailment of international private credit, the need for mutual support among central banks of developing countries will be on the increase.

12. Another significant omission from the programme concerns collective guarantees for investments and loans. The need for such guarantees has been stressed frequently in the past by spokesmen and writers from the surplus developing countries. The absence of guarantees in the Caracas programme may be an omission; but it may also reflect a recently growing view that the inter-country differences, including those between developed and developing countries, in perceived security of investments, are becoming smaller.

13. An important potential inconsistency is built into the Caracas programme. On the one hand, there is the objective,

explicit or implicit, of creating financial institutions of developing countries only, for trade financing, development financing and balance of payments support; all these new institutions will need capital. On the other hand, there is the recommendation to expand the capital of existing regional development banks, in which membership is joint with developed countries and control is shared. Developing countries do not have the resources to provide capital resources for both the proposed new institutions and for the expansion of the existing ones. This conflict will have to be resolved soon.

14. The Caracas programme represents an agreed compromise base for further negotiations among developing countries. In these negotiations, the different country groups will inevitably have different interests. But there is a significant element of mutuality in these national views and interests; and it is these mutual interests that will have to be maximized in the final outcome. This was taken as the guiding principle in preparing the documentation for the Jamaica meeting discussed below.

II Jamaica documentation

Scope

15. The Jamaica Expert Group handled both the balance of payments and the development finance aspects of a possible financial co-operation, in accordance with the Caracas terms of reference. Hence the documentation for the meeting was designed to meet this twin operational objective. The Cuddy paper on commodity finance and the Abbate papers on support of regional credit arrangements and payments arrangements for oil imports refer mainly to the balance of payments support requirements. The Cuddy paper on joint ventures, the Abbate paper on energy investment finance and the Kelkar on investment guarantees refer mainly to the development finance needs. The export credit studies by Cuddy and Tran-Nguyen fall between the two sets of requirements.

16. The Jamaica Expert Group was called upon to advise on the future of the Non-Aligned Solidarity Fund and to consider the earlier proposals for the establishment of a bank for developing countries. Hence the historical background needed to be

provided. The studies by de Silva and Stamenkovic give the history of the Third World efforts at multilateral financial co-operation. Furthermore, a part of the living history is the large ongoing flow of assistance from OPEC to non-OPEC countries, in recognition of the special difficulties experienced by the latter; this is analysed in the Qaqaya paper.

Joint and mutual interests

17. The principle of joint and mutual interests seems to emerge from the Caracas document and spokesmen of both the surplus and the deficit developing countries have announced it on several occasions. For the deficit countries, in the majority, the most urgent issue now and in the foreseeable future is the immediate balance of payments situation, which can be alleviated in different ways. For the surplus countries, the most important elements are the long-run profitability of investments in real terms, and the moderation of the rise in their import prices. For both groups of countries, expansion of exports and of joint investments, coupled with technology transfer, are of major significance. The task is to devise schemes in a fashion which the potential creditors will find acceptable, while meeting the needs of both the debtors and the creditors.

18. The surplus countries have shown considerable interest, in principle, in promoting direct investment and joint ventures in the deficit developing countries, but the machinery for identifying and organizing such investments has been lacking and little has been done in this regard so far. Furthermore, all oil-exporting countries, whether surplus or not, are also interested in other measures which may expand the availability of goods and services in international trade, as they are major and over the long run growing importers of a wide range. Finally, again over the long run, the returns to capital in the developing economies will probably be higher, and their markets, for petroleum and other goods, will be growing faster than in the industrializing countries. These two phenomena are already under way, at least in parts of the developing world, and hence they will be an attractive area for investment by the surplus developing countries.

An IFC study reveals that the discounted cash flow rate of return earned by the IFC (International Finance Corporation) on its equity portfolio was about 10.5 per cent in U.S. dollars between 1961 and 1976, which compared favourably with the 7.75 per cent average annual return that could have been earned by investing in the 425 stocks included in Standard and Poors' industrial average over the same period. The IFC study analyzed the financial data for 87 LDC diverse sector enterprises regarding the rate of return on net worth, and revealed that the median return was 20.5 per cent, the arithmetic average return was 24.8 per cent, and the weighted average return was 21 per cent. Comparatively, the median return on net worth of the 500 largest industrial companies in the United States was a little over 11 per cent during the same period and the average return on net worth of the 425 firms in the Standard and Poor industrial average was 13 per cent.[3]

19. A more recent IFC study, for 1976–80, prepared for a seminar sponsored by IFC and Salomon Brothers, New York, to explore the possibility of developing a 'Third World Equity Fund', also shows higher returns for selected countries: for five of these, the median annual return, adjusted for currency changes, was 33.7 per cent, compared with 9.3 per cent for the US. The IFC warns that 'the data supporting this conclusion are, of course, problematical', although 'they seem to show a relationship between high rates of economic growth and total return on investment in equity securities.'[4] The rates of growth have been higher, on the average, in developing countries during the 1970s.

20. In the deficit countries, the urgency of balance of payments assistance results from the need to help them adjust to the enormous deterioration in the terms of exchange they have experienced in recent years: a sharp decline in their export commodity prices, an upswing in their import prices, particularly of oil and capital and intermediate goods, and a sharp upward shift in the rate of interest which affects not only their new borrowings but also a significant part of their existing stock of debt contracted on a floating rate basis. These countries are also interested in joint ventures with, and direct investment by, the surplus countries; furthermore, they need organized external assistance for the development of their energy and other mineral resources (the oil-exporting countries are interested in the latter as well); finally, they need support for the expansion

of exports which is almost their only salvation over the medium and long run.

21. Three more fundamental points underlying the documentation need to be made. First, any new mechanism or institution which may emerge from the Jamaica meeting and subsequent work is unlikely to involve concessional lending on any significant scale, at least in the near future. Spokesmen from the OPEC countries have been clear in stating that the existing aid institutions—OPEC Fund for International Development, International Fund for Agricultural Development, IDA, other OPEC and international regional aid agencies and national aid institutions—will continue to be the main vehicles through which soft assistance from the OPEC countries will be channelled to the less fortunate parts of the developing world. It follows that the prospect for the revival of the Non-Aligned Solidarity Fund, a body to distribute concessional resources, is slim—see the de Silva study. And conversely, new institutional mechanisms which may develop will deal essentially in non-concessional funds. In some cases subsidy may be needed for a class of lending, e.g. export credit; and the least developed countries will need it for most of their borrowing. But the source and mechanism of subsidy should not be such as to jeopardize the basic nature of a new insitution that may emerge and specifically its ability to obtain funds from the market and the governments and central banks on competitive terms.

22. Secondly, financial and monetary co-operation among the non-oil developing countries has its tradition, mainly in the form of payments (clearing) and modest reciprocal credit arrangements. This co-operation is likely to increase, not only in reciprocal credit schemes (see para. 11 above), but also in payments arrangements: the absolute scarcity of convertible exchange which is now facing a large number of developing countries is likely to give rise to an upsurge of payments (clearing) arrangements which save in transactions exchange. But for such arrangements to lead to a significant and lasting expansion of trade among developing countries, they must have some financial support from outside, i.e. from surplus developing countries or from international financial institutions or from

a South–South financial institution yet to be established. The reason for this is that most non-oil developing countries are running heavy external deficits; virtually none can afford to extend significant credit to the others under present stringent conditions, even under a clearing arrangement, because of the fear that such credit would result in the expansion of its own imports; and without credit, the room for co-operation is narrow, particularly when differences in economic development are significant. The financial co-operation among developing countries in the foreseeable future virtually inevitably depends directly or indirectly, on the engagement of the surplus OPEC countries.

23. Thirdly, surplus OPEC countries are not all powerful, however, and the funds possibly provided by a new institution they may decide to sponsor cannot be expected to substitute for the commitments of the developed countries. Apart from the principle involved, the surplus OPEC countries are simply not big enough to undertake this burden; nor can they be asked to take the risk of placing their newly generated surpluses in developing countries alone. (Nobody is talking about redistribution of the existing investments.) But what the OPEC countries can be expected to do, in line with their own fundamental beliefs and concerns, is to provide resources, or help that such resources be mobilized, for some of the strategic areas which have been deprived of funds, but which are of critical importance for the improvement of the position of the developing countries of the world economy, while at the same time providing reasonable financial return and security. These are the gaps in the financing structure that need to be filled.

III Gaps in the financing structure

24. We are not the first to have drawn attention to the missing elements in the structure of financing. Their common feature is that they involve difficult and sensitive policy issues in the economic and political relationships between North and South. Whether it is programme lending, or commodity stabilization, or promotion of developing countries' exports, or finance to enable them to co-operate with each

other more effectively—all of these, in their several ways, singly and together, are forms of finance which would enable the poor countries to become more self-reliant and independent participants in a more equitable exchange with the rich countries. Thus they all call for a new approach to decision-making.

These gaps have persisted, partly because the governments of the North have been reluctant to change their practices adequately; partly because the developing countries have not been able to influence critical decisions in international institutions. The quality of the relations between borrowers and creditors is vitally important to the character of financial institutions, and their ability to provide for the needs of their clients; the inequality between borrowers and lenders has made it harder to reach joint agreement and to generate mutual trust.[5]

25. The following gaps in the financing structure could be handled through South–South financial co-operation. A more detailed elaboration is provided in the Abbate–Cuddy papers.

(a) *Joint ventures* of the surplus and deficit developing countries, including a project identification and development facility, their promotion and management as appropriate. Such joint ventures and similar direct investment would cover industry, agriculture and mining, as well as the related infrastructure. In part, this operation might be viewed as somehing like a 'South–South IFC'. It could involve itself either as a direct investor in an approved joint venture, or as a broker bringing together various sources of finance while not engaging its own funds directly. By contrast with the IFC, however, the proposed institution would view its investments in joint ventures as long-term in nature, a publicly-owned and publicly-run holding company. A similar idea by Prof. Z. Mikdashi from the University of Lausanne is described in the paper reviewing the proposals for Third World financing co-operation in this collection; even earlier, in 1979, Dr M. W. Khouja, Economic Adviser of the Kuwait Fund for Arab Economic Development had made this proposal.[6]

The concept of joint ventures, broadly defined, is central to the proposals that have been made in this documentation. It covers joint ventures not only in oil-importing, but also in oil-exporting, countries as they are particularly interested in obtaining technology from industrially more advanced developing countries.

(b) Financing of *energy investment*. The need for it has been identified and generally agreed, even at the Cancun Summit, as the priority area. At the United Nations Conference on New and Renewable Energy Sources in Nairobi, August 1981, a related proposal was made by the Prime Minister of Jamaica for the establishment of a specific institution, necessary for accelerating alternative energy technologies. The Expert Group on Energy of the North-South Round Table, a programme of the Society for International Development, proposed in May 1981 the establishment of a new energy investment bank by OPEC, OECD and other countries, alongside a number of other proposals to increase investment in energy. The best known and most discussed has been the World Bank proposal for an energy affiliate. In its original form it was not easily acceptable to OPEC countries which were expected to provide most of the resources, but felt they were not offered sufficient control. This proposal is now dormant because of the opposition of a major developed country member of the Bank.[7] The revived Brandt Commission, at its meeting in early January 1982, suggested immediate action at 'establishing a new energy agency to finance exploration and development of additional energy sources.'[8] The question is whether the developing countries, oil-exporting and oil-importing, would now be prepared to put forward a specific proposal for the establishment of such an agency to engage in oil, gas and coal and perhaps new sources of energy, covering both the risky exploration and the development phase. Given the size of the investment funds required and the need to assure the required technology, presumably such a proposal would be open to membership by the developed countries. One possibility would be equal capital (equity) shares of the two country groups, with a floating portion to be allocated periodically in relation to the source of loanable funds to the agency. Pending resolution of this issue, the development phase of energy lending could be supported by the South financial institution.

(c) *Export credit* financing, guarantee and insurance. A sea of ink has been used during the last twenty years in proving the need for international public financial support of exports, with only small results. The existing international financing agencies, with the exception of the pioneering effort of the Inter-American Development Bank and IFC in Latin America, have not been prepared to provide export sales finance on either a regional or world basis, although there have been cases of World Bank financing of individual country efforts. (Regional banks' data on country support are not readily available.) Similarly, the efforts at UNCTAD to alleviate an international credit guarantee facility for capital goods, stretching over years, have not been successful. What is now necessary is to break this bottleneck and provide export credit finance, refinance, guarantees and insurance in a measure needed to meet the demand in this priority area, not only for capital goods, but also for other non-traditional products, as well as for traditional exports when they go to new markets or are produced or sold by new sellers and need finance—an important element for the expansion of developing countries' intra-trade. Export credit takes up a considerable portion of individual countries' aggregate monetary expansion; and assistance in this field would help relieve some of the immediate domestic inflationary pressures by enabling the financing of larger imports, in addition to the fundamental contributions to the long-run balance of payments adjustment through export expansion. For the providers of funds, export credit is a profitable and safe business as it is covered by goods in production and shipment; and it is possible to attach to it private commercial banks' funds, domestic as well as those of developed countries, as the BLADEX (Latin American Export Bank) experience has shown. From an economic viewpoint, the expansion of export output and trade would contribute to greater competition and thus have an anti-inflationary effect, of particular importance for the OPEC countries which appear to have experienced an extraordinary increase in their import prices.[9] The expected improvement in their terms of trade, resulting from export expansion originating in non-OPEC developing countries and the associated competitive pressure on other suppliers may justify an interest rate subsidy for export credits. Such assistance would help bring about volume expansion and lower prices. Export credit could well be among the first joint ventures to be financed.

(d) *Commodity finance*. The present situation in export commodity markets of non-oil developing countries is desperate. Prices are at their lowest point in real terms since the Second World War and barely above the bottom of the Great Depression of the 1930s. In the last two years, money prices have fallen some 35 per cent. The effects on investment and future supply of primary products will be disastrous if the present situation continues, with subsequent shortages of primary products threatening any sustained recovery of world industrial production. The failure to conclude individual commodity agreements leads to the conclusion that another approach must be taken: financial intervention at the producers' end or on the market, supported by standby supply controls. It is possible that commercial bank financing could be mobilized for a well-designed and resolutely-implemented scheme, provided the direction and the basic finance is available from a public source. The need for new action in the commodity field is also dictated by structural changes in the world commodity markets, where large-scale mergers of commodity trading and financing firms in developed countries are taking place, with an objective to undertake combined lending—trading and perhaps investment operations.[10] For the developing countries to meet this new situation and perhaps benefit from it and participate in it, a much stronger financial organization on their part is needed. Such financing activities could be profitable if properly done; accompanied by standby supply controls they would be virtually riskless; but they would also need realistic pricing to be sustainable. An early analysis of the original design of the Common Fund for commodities, which had anticipated attracting OPEC funds through the issue of composite commodity certificates, has shown that such financing operations, suitably amended to meet present circumstances, could have such effect.[11] Any commodity finance operations as described here would be supportive of, rather than conflicting with, the operations of the Common Fund which is now being ratified.

(e) *Assistance to regional credit (reserve) arrangements* among developing countries. While both export credit finance and particularly commodity finance would provide balance of payments support to developing countries (the latter would be of critical importance for the African countries in particular), they could not provide complete protection, as their incidence depends in part on random factors of economic structure. An important supplement would be assistance from a central source to the existing and prospective credit (mutual support) arrangements among developing countries. There are now five such arrangements, covering forty-two developing countries. It is proposed that they consider creating a Common Stabilization Fund (CSF) by merging a certain percentage of their own resources with external capital if it could be made available. This would increase the aggregate resources; the CSF could further borrow from public and private sources; and capital surplus developing countries may find it attractive to become lenders to the CSF as its obligations would be jointly guaranteed by the member countries and carry the near-market interest rates. Conditions attached to CSF loans would be mainly related to regional economic co-operation programmes and their implementation; and the availability of such balance of payments facility associated with regional co-operation schemes should act as a powerful catalyst for new initiatives in the field of financial co-operation among developing countries, such as the creation of additional and more ambitious regional credit arrangements. The other affect would be that there would be some relief in the demand for IMF total resources as regional pooling would make for a better use of the countries' own funds. Such a scheme would in fact mean an emerging gradual regionalization of stabilization assistance.

(f) *Payments arrangements for oil imports.* This is a difficult part, in view of the well-known position of most OPEC countries that concessions may result in spoiling the market. Several alternative ways have been suggested in which a moderate relief to the oil-importing countries can be provided. The risk of market spoilage can be reduced to practically zero by providing for automatic suspension of all access to financial co-operative funds in case of manipulation. On the other hand, a special facility, such as payment for a fraction in local currency with maintenance-of-value clause and subsequent use of it for development finance purposes or for OPEC equity investments in joint ventures could have a far-reaching effect on the integration of developing countries and ultimate success of OPEC direct investments.

26. An institution which could handle joint investments, and some of the other functions discussed above, could also perform the functions of a merchant banking facility. It would then have the advantage of participating directly in international capital markets; create new sources of capital, e.g. in the Nordic countries and others with little private involvement in developing countries; and develop sound commercial and financial intelligence, leading to the establishment of capacity to provide a continuing and solid financial and management advice. The importance of developing such capacity should not be underestimated, whether for use by the OPEC or non-OPEC corporations, or governments.

IV Resource availability

27. The resource problem has four aspects. First, the present moment is not particularly propitious for establishing a major new institution. The oil-exporting countries have difficulties in the market: if reminder was needed that in the final analysis all primary producers share similar fortunes, the commodity markets have provided it during the last year. However, the importance of present difficulties should not be exaggerated. It is the surplus OPEC countries which inevitably have to give a lead in financial co-operation among the developing countries if it is to be undertaken on a large scale; and while the current oil revenue and surplus of some of them is sharply down, they are not cash-poor. Large reserves have been built up, and some of them, invested short term, are yielding high interest income at present rates. Nor is the present oil market situation likely to last, judging by all past history. At least an element of it is due to the recession and high interest rates, which force down the inventory holdings making them very expensive, in addition to depressing current users' demand. For the medium term, oil is still the king in the commodity markets and in most other

markets. The uncertainties in nuclear power seem to have reduced severely its competitive threat to oil.[12] Cancellation of some other competitive energy projects works in the same direction. The fact that a major and experienced oil producer has recently embarked on major acquisitions in the same and related fields is an indication that the present situation is not considered as a forerunner of future developments.

28. Secondly, a new institution, if it had full backing of the OPEC states, would probably represent a powerful new factor in the capital markets, able to attract funds which otherwise might be shy. A new institution would have more than one advantage. It would start with a clean slate: many of the existing institutions, private and public, suffer from having their assets and sometimes commitments locked up at relatively low interest rates, while they have to mobilize new funds at interest rates sometimes twice as high. The resulting pressure on profits of some banks has been severe. If the new insitution is prudently run, it would have in a way the best of both worlds: debtors who consider it their own, and major shareholders who are the main, if not the only, creditors in the world.[13] Ultimately, of course, the credibility of the new institution will depend on its portfolio.

29. Thirdly, in the long run, the institution will depend as much on the oil-importing as on the oil-exporting countries, not only as debtors but also as shareholders. The surplus oil-exporting countries have a very narrow resource base; they are in fact transforming one asset, oil, into another, cash and investments; but once oil runs out, they will depend on the skills they have developed and on the soundness of the investments they have made. The oil-importing countries with wide natural resource bases are in a more fortunate long-run position, however paradoxical this may sound from the present vantage point. These factors should be reflected, in some inventive way, in the capital structure of any new institution which may be set up.

30. Fourthly, even over the short run, there has to be cost-sharing between the surplus and the deficit countries. Both groups of countries need to participate not only in the subscribed, but also in the paid-up capital, although in different

proportions. Universal participation, or as universal as possible allowing for the poorest, in the paid-up capital is probably the only solid basis on which an institution of this kind can be built. But it should be added that the 'cost' and 'cost-sharing' are misnomers in the case of establishing a bank. If it is set up right and if it is run as a viable institution capable of borrowing on the capital market, there is no cost to the founders, only an investment. Those who need the funds would be able to borrow for acceptable projects in amounts greater than they have put in; and all shareholders would earn income on capital. It is in a sense a costless operation; but it calls for a commitment of future liability if things go wrong and for an initial, although modest, outlay of capital.

V Institutional issues

31. The work has not advanced to the point at which firm institutional suggestions can be made. What seems clear is that energy investment will have to be treated separately from the rest: it seems to be generally agreed that energy is a North-South responsibility in which both sides have vital interests.

32. With respect to the rest—joint ventures holding company, export credit support, commodity market finance, support from reserve credit arrangements, handling of return flow on any possible fractional arrangement concerning oil payments if it can be agreed at all, merchant banking facility—more than one solution is possible. Advantages of specialization exist in having a different institution for each class of operations; but even greater advantages may exist in having one all-embracing powerful body with flexibility in resource mobilization and use.

33. An important issue is the relationship of any new institution to the OPEC Fund for International Development. The OPEC countries are rightly proud of its achievements, methods of operation and reputation and prestige. In a sense, OPEC Fund is a soft lending agency of the South: it is the IDA of the South. It has provided balance of payments support when it has been critically needed, and its project lending is heavily oriented towards energy. It is difficult to envisage the new institution, or institutions, which would by their nature handle non-concessionary

lending and investing, being incorporated into a transformed OPEC Fund; but it is also difficult to envisage building something entirely new and separate from the OPEC Fund. A thought necessarily crosses one's mind that what may be needed is a South Bank Group, in which OPEC Fund would continue as a major soft lending agency, with its own capital structure; while the rest would be built new—a South Bank—and would stand parallel. Both institutions, or even more than two, would share the experiences and common services and facilities. These are only random thoughts, however, and much thinking and work will have to be done before different alternatives are spelled out in detail, together with their implications. What needs to be done first is to decide whether there is a case at all for any new institution. If such a case is agreed, there is much to be said for a South Bank which simultaneously handles both the development finance and the balance of payments lending. The experience has shown that this is necessary. It can thus help achieve some of the objectives of the Iraqi proposal of 1979—see para. 10 above.

34. Any new institution which may be established should be expected to work in close co-operation with the existing financing agencies, regional and interregional. It will also have to work closely with banks and producing and marketing firms in the developed countries. Joint ventures will frequently involve multinational companies from the developed countries. Export credit will be needed for exports to developed countries as well as to developing ones, although the latter trade may be the major beneficiary. Both export credit and commodity finance should use the resources and expertise of the developed countries' banks. In many operations there will be relations, exchange of views and participation in joint projects with the IFC, World Bank Group, regional development banks and others. In balance of payments support, there will be need for co-operation in data exchange and analysis with the IMF.

35. The idea to establish a South Bank as a major powerful lending institution inevitably dominates one's thinking of financial co-operation among developing countries. For it to become a reality, major financial support is needed from the surplus countries, but also a substantial equity stake needs to

be forthcoming from the deficit countries. Also needed would be a co-ordinating forum of developing countries which would include the interested countries and agencies and provide an organized framework for discussion of joint approaches on issues of monetary and financial co-operation.

VI Implications for the reconstruction of the international financial and monetary system

36. The establishment of a South Bank as a major institution would have three implications for the future international system. First, by providing major additional capacity for project identification, selection, assessment, underwriting and financing, it might add new quality to international investment finance. Capacity of this kind would be particularly important at the present juncture, in the light of the need to convert some of the existing international debt into equity (share capital) holdings. Such equities, assuming they are profitable, can be taken over by the South Bank or through it for the benefit of the investors in surplus developing countries, at an appropriate price. Precedents for such possible arrangements exist, the latest successful one in Turkey, and the other one now possibly developing in some Latin American countries. The potential benefits for all concerned could be large; the debtor countries would scale down fixed obligations which are now a major burden, the banks would obtain cash which they badly need, their creditors–depositors would be relieved of some of their concerns, and the new direct investors (which in some cases may be the creditors–depositors of banks) would acquire productive assets.

37. Secondly, if a South Bank were to get involved in country stabilization operations, a new view of conditionality may emerge. It may help the present one which still essentially operates by reducing demand and thus contributes to deflation in the international system both when circumstances justify such deflationary pressures and when they do not—as at present. The surplus countries are now tacit partners in these efforts as they help supply the funds which are being lent for stabilization. In fact, their interests are very much in the direction of expansion of foreign demand for oil, which is in trouble like many other commodities, and for other products.

38. Thirdly, a South Bank may be instrumental in the widening and deepening of the Arabian Gulf capital market by offering a satisfactory volume and range of debt instruments; and should their monetary authorities find this acceptable and attractive, an entirely new prospect may be in the offing of security issues in Gulf country currencies. This may have significant implications for the international monetary system, the role of developing countries, and particularly Saudi Arabia, in it, and the future pricing and payments regime for oil. While the Gulf countries have resisted the prospect of their currencies becoming international currencies thus far, the enormous fluctuations of the present reserve currencies, and the associated fluctuations in the international price of oil as it actually affects the different national markets in the world, are inevitably forcing a re-examination of policy on oil pricing and payments of the major producers. It is not possible to control the price of oil under present circumstances. Either the international monetary system would evolve in the direction of an international currency under co-ordinated international control, or there would be further growth and diversity of national reserve currency standards, including probably the Gulf. In either case, growth of the money and capital markets in the Gulf is likely, and a South financial institution could play a role in it more satisfactorily than the national or regional institutions. It would imply sharing of control, but it would also mean diversification of risks, which ought to be of high value.

Notes

1. All paragraph references refer to the text of the Caracas Decisions distributed to the United Nations (A/36/333) on 26 June 1981.
2. Typing error in the original text; it should read 24e.
3. Arjun Sengupta, *The Structure of International Finance and the Less Developed Economies*, United Nations, New York, 1977, pp. 58-9 (mimeo).
4. Presentation by the International Financial Corporation on portfolio investment in the Third World, through a Third World Equity Fund, organized by Salomon Brothers and IFC, 16 September 1981. (Communication by IFC of 23 December 1981.)
5. *North-South, A Programme for Survival,* The Report of the Independent Commission on International Development Issues under the Chairmanship of Willy Brandt, London, 1980, p. 236. The Commission

Secretariat Paper 'International Financial System and Institutions' of 2 February 1979, which served as the basis of the above text, had also listed two additional gaps in the financing structure: development of mineral resources to the advantage of developing countries, and reorganization of unviable debt structures. (See the *Brandt Commission Papers*, Geneva–The Hague, 1981, p. 609.)

6. Communication to the Brandt Commission Secretariat in the letter of 12 March 1979.
7. See the statements of Mr Clausen, President of the Bank, in Washington, D.C., on 16 December 1981, and in New Delhi on 21 January 1982, as reported by the *Inter-Press Service* of 18 December and *Financial Times* of 23 January.
8. Press statement, Kuwait, 9 January 1982.
9. This has led to the view in OPEC countries that a reorientation of their investment policy may provide a brake against world inflation and therefore against the erosion of the import purchasing power of OPEC exports and of OPEC savings. It is argued that the mere placements (deposits and purchases of financial instruments) of OPEC funds in developed countries, which do not represent new real investments, could easily lead to a loss in the real value of these assets. Investing the funds in new real investments in the developing countries, where they have their greatest potential, and presumably in their associated export trade, would, on the other hand, protect their real value, while adding to the real wealth of the world and discouraging inflation. See I. F. I. Shihata, *Some Prerequisites for the North-South Dialogue*, the OPEC Fund for International Development, Vienna, 1981, p. 22.
10. This is in particular the case with the merger in mid-1981 of the two powerful Wall Street firms, Philip Brothers, commodity traders, and Salomon Brothers, a securities firm, resulting in a combined capital of US $1.5 billion. Both firms are US-registered, but Philip Brothers is 28 per cent owned by Mineral Resources Corporation (Minorco), a Bermuda-based company, owned by South African interests (Oppenheimer) which have a major influence on the international metal market and largely control the international diamond market.
11. Mohamad W. Khouja, *Capital Structure and Financing of the Common Fund for Financing Commodity Stocks*, Institute for Development, Vienna, 14–18 February 1977.
12. It is reported that in 1981 only two reactors obtained authorization to enter production in the US, while six projects were cancelled and forty-four slowed down. For the third year in a row, following the Three Mile Island accident in March 1979, no new construction permit has been issued. Moody's Investors Service has been reducing the credit rating of power plants being built in Washington State,

citing uncertainty surrounding the fate of the projects. (*International Herald Tribune* of 8 January and *Journal de Genève* of 21 January 1982.)

13. During 1974–80, the industrial countries ran a cumulative current account deficit in their balances of payments of US $20 billion, and the oil-exporting developing countries a cumulative surplus of US $357 billion. (I. S. Gulati, *Failure of International Monetary Reform: Scope for South–South Initiatives*, New Delhi, 27 February 1982.) In 1981, the high-income oil-exporting countries ran a surplus of US $76 billion, and in 1982 an estimated US $35 billion, compared to surpluses of industrial market economies of US $2 billion in 1981 and an estimated US $15 billion in 1982. (World Bank, *World Development Report 1982*.)

2 THE NON-ALIGNED MOVEMENT AND THE GROUP OF 77—ISSUES IN MONETARY AND FINANCIAL CO-OPERATION, WITH A CASE STUDY OF THE NON-ALIGNED SOLIDARITY FUND FOR ECONOMIC AND SOCIAL DEVELOPMENT

LEELANANDA DE SILVA

Part I

The strengthening of economic co-operation among developing countries (ECDC) is a primary objective of both the Non-Aligned Movement (NAM) and the Group of 77 (G.77). Indeed, in the case of the NAM, it is the major rationale of its economic component, as expressed in the Action Programmes adopted at successive conferences. The G.77 is more concerned with the organization of a countervailing power, in its manifestation as the 'South', in North–South negotiations and, to that extent, less concerned with the evolution of intra-Southern co-operation, though by no means does it imply an absence of involvement in ECDC. The G.77 must be involved for two very good reasons—first, it is a wider grouping than NAM and has to develop NAM concerns on ECDC within this wider setting, and second, the G.77 with its UN base must utilize to the fullest extent the capacity available within international organizations (in particular UNCTAD) to promote ECDC.

Over the last two decades, an astonishing variety of proposals have been envisaged for ECDC or South–South co-operation encompassing every possible sector of a country's economy. The question might be relevantly posed whether it is the proliferation of schemes which have resulted in the extremely slow progress made in their implementation. A more refined and selective agenda might have yielded a better outcome. This paper will be concerned with the sector on money and finance and a brief survey of the developments in that sector is envisaged. The UNCTAD discussions on ECDC, which involve issues within a North–South context, are not considered, and as for intra-South forms of co-operation, the agenda is in any case shaped by the G.77 and NAM.

Organs of co-operation

Before such a survey, a short digression. The NAM and the G.77 are not the only forums within which proposals are made and negotiations undertaken for South–South monetary and financial co-operation. There are other theatres and other actors, though not always as 'global' as the NAM and the G.77. Four other broad groups of institutions might be noted.

1. The Group of 24, which is in fact an adjunct of the G.77 but yet having an almost autonomous existence and concerned more with the negotiating function for the South *vis-à-vis* the North. Its main activity is within the Bretton Woods institutions and has very little to do with the rest of the UN system. The G.24 is strongly representative of Ministries of Finance and Central Banks and is concerned primarily with the operation of the international monetary system and its possible re-definition. Almost no proposals have been made for an independent strengthening of developing countries' monetary and financial institutions in the context of ECDC.[1]
2. Regional and subregional institutions either established or envisaged, for greater monetary and financial co-operation among some developing countries. This category has expanded subtantially over the last two decades and it is not expected to list them here. They include clearing unions and payments arrangements (for example, the Asian Clearing Union (1974), the Central American Clearing House (1961) and so on), and various networks and conferences of Central Banks meeting either regularly for consultations or at annual conferences. There is also, for example, the African Monetary Institute. These are institutions which could be made use of for developing a more intensive degree of regional and subregional co-operation and their work, though of great significance to NAM and G.77, are not normally the subject of the latter's deliberations. A point to be considered is whether the NAM and the G.77 at regular intervals should at least not review the progress made by this type of organization as they all

promote South–South co-operation in the most practical manner.

3. Though not distinct from category (2) above, it is relevant to identify separately the emergence of a range of financial and monetary institutions with close links with some of the OPEC and more particularly OAPEC countries. To name but a few at random—the Islamic Development Bank, the Arab Bank for Economic Development in Africa, the Arab Monetary Fund and the Arab Fund for Economic and Social Development could be included. A strong transnational monetary and financial network encompassing an important group of developing countries has thus been created. They are organizations that wield considerable financial power and cater to a substantial number of developing countries. An important issue here is also the effect subregional and regional networks have on more global types of NAM and G.77 co-operation. Will, for example, intensive forms of co-operation arrangements within ASEAN in monetary and financial matters dampen their enthusiasm for broader enterprises? If so, what is the division of labour between the regional and subregional groups and the more global NAM and G.77?
4. Regional institutions such as the regional commissions of the UN and organizations like OAU and SELA, whose concerns are much wider than financial and monetary issues, but nevertheless constitute breeding grounds for ideas and concepts for regional monetary and financial co-operation. As an illustration, ESCAP was the progenitor of both the Asian Development Bank, the Asian Clearing Union and the Asian Reserve Bank, the latter not seeing the light of day. These regional institutions have a continuing important role in seeking the implementation at a regional level of proposals for South–South co-operation. It is a matter for some reflection as to why regional economic commissions, which are in the habit of convening regional conferences prior to most major UN conferences, avoid doing so in relation to the more powerful cousins of the UN system—the IMF and IBRD and their annual conferences. It is a subject which deserves some consideration, particularly in view of the fact that some developing countries do meet together, though not exclusively, in forums like

the Commonwealth Finance Ministers Conference, and even more because of the strong regional orientation of institutional monetary and financial policy.

The four broad groups of institutions mentioned above constitute a framework for strengthening NAM and G.77 co-operation. Along with NAM and G.77 they are the forums for developing countries to strengthen their monetary and financial relationships. Rather than wait for the day of creating global developing countries institutions, it might be useful and more practical to examine how existing institutions can be strengthened and linkages among them increased. Such a task could be appropriate for both NAM and G.77. For effective performance, NAM and G.77 will have to take note of developments in the above four groups and act as a kind of co-ordinator.[2]

The formative years

Within the NAM and the G.77, several proposals have been made for financial and monetary co-operation. Before a brief assessment of their rationale and feasibility is made, it might be in order to see the gradual evolution of ideas during the early years of NAM interest in economic issues.

The NAM probably has its origins in the Bandung Conference of 1955. From that time until 1972, when the Georgetown Conference of Foreign Ministers was held, the NAM concerns in monetary and financial matters in the context of ECDC was confined to the elaboration of ideas of a more general nature rather than the formulation of proposals for any specific institution. In Bandung, there is very little reference, apart from calling for the enlargement of the scope for 'multilateral trade and payments' and 'the establishment of national and regional banks and insurance companies.'[3] At the first Non-Aligned Summit in Belgrade in 1961, there was hardly any reference to ECDC issues. At the Special Conference of Developing Countries, on the Problems of Economic Development, held in Cairo in 1962, the Declaration issued after the Conference constitutes essentially a programme for international economic reform. ECDC in terms of strengthening intra-developing country monetary and financial links is virtually non-existent. Hindsight would probably affirm the view that the 1960s were the years of benevolence of the rich industrialized countries and the age of belief in incremental reform (UNCTAD I and so on). In 1970, at the Third Non-Aligned Summit held in Lusaka, monetary and financial issues of an ECDC nature are limited to the call 'to evolve payment arrangements to support expansion of trade exchanges amongst developing countries.' The picture is no different in the G.77 at the time of the First Ministerial Meeting and the Charter of Algiers in 1967. All financial and monetary issues were related to the IMF, IBRD, UNCTAD and bilateral aid and no mention made of ECDC.[4]

The Georgetown Action Programme of the NAM in 1972 constitutes a watershed in the evolution of the concept of ECDC.[5] In money and finance, it called for clearing and payments arrangements, the establishment of 'correspondent' banking relations among national commercial banks, and co-ordination of arrangements relating to export credits, exchange control policies within integrated groupings, and common foreign investment policies. Though these constitute new initiatives, they are modest in scope and do not envisage necessarily the creation of any new institutions. What was hoped for were new kinds of machinery for consultation and not intergovernmental organizations. Georgetown, however, was preceded by a meeting of a Committee of Economic Experts and their report is of a pioneering nature in NAM history.[6] The proposals above were based on the work of the Experts. There was also the appointment of a Committee on Direct Foreign Investment which later reported to the Algiers Summit, having met in Santiago, Chile a week prior to the overthrow of the Allende regime. The report was heavily influenced by the atmosphere of the time in Chile and of the unacceptable face of TNCs. An important recommendation was consistency of legislation on direct foreign investment.

The years 1972–3 witnessed intense activity in the design of an NAM Economic Action Programme, particularly in the period prior to the Non-Aligned Summit in Algiers in September 1973, held only weeks before the major increase in oil prices by OPEC. Georgetown had appointed India and Indonesia as co-ordinators for monetary and financial co-operation, and in a paper presented jointly by them to the Algiers Summit detailed proposals were set forth for a system of clearing arrangements at an intra-regional level, a payments arrangement either in the form of a Payments Union or a Reseive Fund and a Project Development Facility. The paper constitutes the first detailed elaboration of co-operative arrangements among non-aligned and other developing countries in the financial and monetary sector. As it stated,

> The paper is to highlight the significance, scope and potentialities that exist for co-operation in the monetary and financial fields among non-aligned countries. The growth of such co-operation will contribute to the achievement of their overall economic and socio-political objectives. This paper is prepared in the form of a base document providing the broad concepts of proposals that can be analysed, and perhaps spelt out in greater detail through debate and discussion.[7]

This paper and the Algiers Summit of 1973 mark the beginning of the successive proposals for the creation of new institutions in money and finance. Hitherto, institutions had been considered at subregional and regional levels, but from now on what is envisaged is broader in scope, encompassing the non-aligned and the developing countries. The South was born in an organic sense and no longer limited to the trade union function of negotiating with the North. One could state that self-help, self-reliance, and collective self-reliance as operational concepts were now integrated with the negotiating function. It might be noted that this aspect of ECDC, in its organic sense, and creating an autonomous South goes back less than ten years. It dates from Georgetown and Algiers (1972–3).

The Algiers Summit, apart from endorsing the proposals referred to above, added several others. It hinted at the possibility of a joint financial institution between the central banks of developing countries. On the basis of a proposal made by Kuwait, the Summit adopted a special resolution on the establishment of an Economic and Social Development Fund for Non-Aligned Countries. The Solidarity Fund thus constitutes a landmark in proposals for institutionalization within the NAM and the G.77, and the latter part of the paper will consequently elaborate in some detail on the evolution of this proposal.

Algiers and after

The period 1973–6 constitutes a distinctive period in the evolution of the economic thinking of the NAM and the G.77. The immediate aftermath of the Algiers Summit witnessed the newly-acquired power of OPEC in determining the price of oil, and the strong support extended to OPEC by the developing countries. The new strength of OPEC had several consequences for the developing countries. One was the prospect of emulation, by other commodity producers and hence the Conference on Raw Materials of Developing Countries held in Dakar in 1975.[8] A new financial institution—A Common Fund of the Developing Countries—was proposed and adopted at Dakar. It was dependent on substantial resources forthcoming from the OPEC countries. This was the second consequence. The NAM and G.77 started to think in terms of institutions which could assist in the channelling of OPEC surpluses to other developing countries. Initially, the emphasis was on concessionary funds and during this period such a tendency was buttressed by the limited absorptive capacity of OPEC states. This, however, was a temporary phenomenon. Moreover, the concessionary channels were created outside the framework of NAM and G.77; in the OPEC Fund controlled by the OPEC members, the Islamic Development Bank, the Arab Fund for Economic and Social Development (though created in 1973, it became functional only in 1974), and in the International Fund for Agricultural Development which for an international financial agency provided for a new voting structure favouring the developing countries.

These years brought a new sense of strength to developing countries; the two special sessions of the UN General Assembly and the adoption of the NIEO resolutions and the Charter of Economic Rights and Duties of States. Collective self-reliance and ECDC emerged as operationally relevant concepts and a gradual merger was evident as between the Action Programmes on Economic Co-operation of the G.77 and the NAM each overlapping with the other. The best illustration of this tendency is to be found in the Action Programmes on Economic Co-operation adopted at Manila, Colombo and Mexico all in 1976 in that order, the first and last being G.77 meetings and the Colombo Meeting being the Fifth Non-Aligned Summit. In the monetary and financial field, these trends were reflected in the decisions of the Colombo Summit to establish a Bank of the Developing Countries, a countervailing currency and a Developing Countries' Payments Union. The period 1973–6 was extremely productive in terms of new institutions in the South—but not within G.77 and NAM.

A new realism

Since 1977, the worsening of the balance of payments of most developing countries and the gradual erosion of the surpluses of most oil-exporting countries have introduced an urgent note of realism to G.77 and NAM deliberations. The scope for concessional flows among developing countries appears to be limited though the potential for increased flows of non-concessional funds appear to be substantial. The few developing countries which have a financial surplus for investment appear to be more keen to diversify their investment and channel a significant portion of the available funds to developing countries provided remunerative outlets are offered for this purpose. Consequently, mechanisms for such a task need to be devised. There is also the potential for increased trade co-operation within the South and collaboration in various ventures in industry, agriculture, transport and so on. These, too, demand financial mechanisms among participating countries. It is these imperatives which presently shape the NAM and G.77 agenda in monetary and financial sectors of ECDC, and the 1977 meeting of the NAM Co-ordinator Countries held in Belgrade set out in some detail an agenda for future action. The meeting agreed to establish two working groups, one for the promotion of Central Bank co-operation and the other for promotion of co-operation among commercial banks. Apart from co-operation among these fraternal institutions, and the exchange of information on bank credit and access to capital markets, the meeting urged the expert investigation of the following proposals:

(a) The feasibility of a countervailing currency backed by the economic potential of developing countries;
(b) the establishment of a joint financial institution for the promotion of financial and monetary co-operation among developing countries;
(c) the establishment of a Developing Countries Payment Union;
(d) the feasibility of mechanisms required to create a unit of liquidity to be used exclusively among the developing countries;
(e) to strengthen existing clearing arrangements and the creation

of new ones at the subregional, regional and interregional levels;

(f) establishing links among existing payments schemes and the creation of subregional, regional and interregional payments arrangements;

(g) harmonization of exchange rate policies for the promotion of intra-developing country trade;

(h) establishment and operation of a Bank of the Developing Countries which would undertake the general activities of commercial and merchant banking;

(i) the operation of interest subsidy schemes; and

(j) additional arrangements for export credit and export credit guarantee schemes to help finance intra-developing country trade.[9]

This is a broad agenda and it was evident at the Non-Aligned Summit held in Havana in late 1979 that not much progress has been made with the required studies and research. The position has not changed appreciably even at the end of 1981.[10] The NAM and the G.77 are obviously handicapped by a dearth of institutional support and there is tremendous scope for useful intervention through technical assistance to help overcome the present impasse. The High-Level Conference on Economic Co-operation among Developing Countries held in Caracas in May 1981 also adopted an agenda for the monetary and financial sector, which in many ways resembles the 1977 Belgrade agenda and here again there is a lack of movement in meeting commitments and deadlines.

This chapter has not analysed every communiqué and every Action Programme of the NAM and G.77 relevant to ECDC in the monetary and financial sector. These communiqués and Action Programmes largely overlap each other. One of the more easily implementable suggestions worth consideration is the adoption by the forthcoming Seventh Non-Aligned Summit in Delhi of a definitive action programme in the monetary and financial sector, taking note of all previous proposals, and agreeing on a nomenclature which could subsequently be adhered to by developing countries, whenever they meet, under whatever manifestation—NAM, G.77 or any other regional and interregional grouping.

A programme for the future

The brief historical description of NAM and G.77 action in the ECDC money and finance sector provides some indication of the rationale for co-operation. Monetary and financial co-operation is not dependent on the existence of financial surpluses among a few developing countries. Its imperative lies in the need to create a monetary and financial infrastructure within the South which would facilitate trade, aid, investment and other forms of co-operative economic endeavour to expedite the economic and social development of these countries. The OPEC surpluses of the 1970s only spotlighted the massive dependence of developing countries—capital-surplus or capital-deficient—on the financial and monetary infrastructure of the North. The developing countries were dependent either as creditors or as debtors on Northern transnational banks, the IMF and Northern governments. Monetary and financial co-operation within the South could bring gains to all developing countries by reducing such dependence and creating a more balanced international structure in money and finance. It is a long and difficult journey over unexplored terrain. In any assessment of an individual project, note must therefore be taken of the contribution it makes in creating this new infrastructure. The NAM and G.77 agenda in this sector is already determined and must continue to be determined from this angle.

With the overall background in mind, it is proposed to set out below very briefly a few considerations to be noted consequent on the availability of financial surpluses among some developing countries, and the increased financial and economic strength of several others. These considerations, it is felt, should influence the G.77 and NAM in formulating their strategy.

OPEC countries have emerged as substantial donors of concessionary funds and this trend must be encouraged to the greatest possible extent. The problems of low-income developing countries need particular attention. There has been a tendency on the part of some of the industrialized countries, and even of OECD, to refer to the heavy concentration of OPEC countries' concessionary funds on a few countries of consequence to them in their own regions. This is contrasted with the OECD practice of a wider geographical disbursement of funds. The implied criticism of developing country donors must be contradicted for two reasons. OECD and OPEC are not comparable. The first is a group of over twenty countries (DAC) which are the world's richest, and OPEC is an amalgam with some of the world's poorest countries thrown in. What should be compared is the country specificity of individual OECD and OPEC member countries. Australia, for example, directs 56 per cent of its aid budget to Papua New Guinea and 82 per cent on the developing countries of South East Asia and the South Pacific. Half the total disbursements of Canadian aid is concentrated on twelve countries. Over half of French aid is targeted towards its overseas Departments and Territories and, indeed, 87 per cent is allocated to Francophone countries. In the case of the USA, there is a similar concentration of aid.[11] The concentration of OPEC aid on a regional basis is no better or worse than similar considerations which determine the pattern of distribution of aid by several OECD countries. This point is of importance to the G.77 and NAM as it must be their responsibility too to create a network of financial, monetary and economic relationships which would provide the necessary incentives for wider distribution of concessionary funds. The failure of the Solidarity Fund for Social and Economic Development to take off is a particular illustration of the weak response of recipient developing countries to take appropriate initiatives. The Northern experience of aid distribution also sustains the thesis of the close interaction of development aid with foreign investment and trade. The more a developing country has close economic links—through investment, the purchase of equipment and machinery or as a commodity supplier—the more the possibility of aid either direct or in a more disguised form (for example, the United Kingdom's governmental subsidy on its export credits is £500 million annually—nearly half what the UK spends on aid). The point to be stressed is that the longer term continuance of concessionary flows from developing donor countries will of necessity be linked to their perceived economic and strategic interests and it is the task of the NAM and G.77 to assist in the creation of a non-ethnic, extra-regional network of economic interdependence. This is a task which has yet to be undertaken seriously by these institutions.

The successful creation of such a network demands close

integration among sectoral activities of the G.77 and NAM. Industry, trade, shipping and commodities have substantial monetary and financial implications and it is not evident that the present arrangement of work within the NAM and G.77, tightly compartmentalized for each sector, is conducive to a greater integration of approach. There is possibly a case for across-the-sector task forces on clearly assigned programmes. Two possible programmes, out of a large number which can be envisaged, are in shipping and commodities.

In shipping there is the potential for greater involvement by developing countries and several permutations and combinations for joint ventures, either bilateral or multilateral, appear to be economically feasible. The capital-surplus countries could provide the down-payment finance, and the other developing country parties could assure a share of their trade and cargo. Inter-governmental negotiations cannot always bring about these linkages, and herein lies the case for a Commercial and Merchant Bank of the developing countries, which could mobilize the potential which exists on the basis of commercial criteria. The NAM and G.77 must create structures which facilitate this kind of commercial deal among developing countries. It happens most of the time between developing and developed, and the capital which finances such projects is not always from the developed countries.

The second feasible programme is in commodity development—in the processing, marketing, shipping and distribution of commodities. These are activities which presently take place mostly outside the borders of commodity-producing countries —in countries in the North which constitute the markets for these commodities. Depending on the commodity, the costs of downstream involvement are substantial, but commodity producers could capture substantial gains if they could control a larger share of their commodity transaction beyond the mere production of the raw commodity. The possible gains have been worked out elsewhere but what needs to be noted here is the potential for joint investments in these downstream operations by commodity-producing and capital-surplus countries. It could, for example, be in a cocoa- or coffee-processing plant. The commodity-producing country has the advantage accruing to it from controlling the supply of the commodity at source and some expertise. The capital-surplus country will be provided with a remunerative outlet for its investment in a venture that will not raise the usual problem of guarantees on investment as the investment could itself be located in a developed country or in the investors' country itself. This could also be the case in the joint shipping ventures referred to above, as location need not be in a poor developing country without access to guarantees. There is the added advantage that this type of investment does not require 'new' projects but merely the takeover and, if necessary, the expansion of existing enterprises in the North. The capital-surplus developing countries have already encountered resistance to their growing investments in the North and association with other developing countries in investments in the latter's traditional industries will to some extent obviate such a circumstance. It might in time be even feasible to re-deploy some of these industries or even some parts in the chain of processing. It is not possible here to explore in detail the feasibility even in a general way for joint enterprises in commodity development. Within the UNCTAD's Integrated Programme for Commodities, commodity development is now emerging as a key issue, and the NAM and G.77, in the context of ECDC, could explore this particular issue from its investment dimension treating it more as a financial rather than a commodity support or control question.[12]

Another related issue in terms of diverting a part of the surplus capital of some developing countries to be used by other developing countries is the role of international monetary institutions. Some of the surplus developing countries have had recourse already to the facilities offered both by the IMF and the World Bank. They have made available funds to these two institutions for onward transmission to developing countries. These institutions consequently have emerged to an extent as intermediaries in South–South transactions. At least in such a context, if not in the overall administrative management and control of the institutions, more power over decision-making could be justifiably exercised by the developing countries. The IMF itself has provided a special facility for the Group of 10 countries in the form of their General Agreement to Borrow (GAB). Though the swap facilities under the arrangement are between each other, it is the IMF which is the intermediary. Similar facilities for South–South transactions, modified to suit the circumstances, could be evolved. The IMF would constitute the intermediary in such a situation. The idea would be to use the IMF more intensively for South–South transactions, and controlled in that limited work more by developing countries, if that is possible. The question must be further explored to identify the IMF's role in ECDC, at least in the promotion of trade, which fits in with its philosophy and as a counter to Northern protectionism. The IMF now is essentially an organ for the economic management of developing countries, and has only a peripheral influence on the Northern countries. The present situation of the capital-surplus developing countries as creditor countries should be reflected more clearly in IMF and World Bank decisions. The bargaining power to achieve such an adjustment within these institutions would lie in the pursuance of exclusive South–South institutions for channelling funds both for development finance and balance of payments needs. The Caracas programme identifies the need for institutions to handle such funds and the G.77 and NAM strategies should be to proceed in both directions.

This raises another question of some importance—the coordination and integration of the ECDC dimension of money and finance (dealt with primarily by the NAM and G.77) and the North–South dimension of international monetary reform (which is G.24 territory). So far, they have proceeded in somewhat autonomous fashion, but the interrelatedness of these two aspects is critical to any success in reforming international monetary institutions. One could illustrate this nexus briefly by looking at World Bank lending policy. The World Bank will not provide resources to a commodity-producing developing country to invest in downstream operations outside its territory—in processing, marketing, shipping or distribution. It was noted above that this is an area for possible future investments. There is no reason whatever, based on economic and not political criteria, why the World Bank should not change its lending policy to allow for funds for downstream investments. This could be facilitated if the funds for this purpose came from capital-surplus developing countries, either through a special 'window' or through the General Account. The shift in the sources of funding of these institutions from industrialized to developing countries must be reflected not only in decision-making structures, but even more so in their lending policies and policies on conditionality and so on, which should take note of the role these institutions should increasingly play in South–South economic intermediation. The rest of the UN system has now a role to play in ECDC, granted the universality principle. So has the IMF and IBRD, particularly because they obtain substantial resources from the South, and are concerned with managing the South rather than the North. From this perspective, the G.77 and the NAM have an urgent task in re-fashioning their strategy along with the G.24 in issues relating to reform of international monetary institutions. It is in the interests of all developing countries and in the interests of these institutions to consider their greater orientation to South–South transactions, and their statutes need not stand in the way so long as the general thrust is towards the expansion of world trade.

One firm conclusion from the above analysis is the urgent need for more research both at a conceptual and empirical level to improve the G.77 and NAM agenda in monetary and financial matters. There are too many loose ends and a major gap in the co-ordination of various proposals. The interrelatedness of the North–South and South–South issues has been inadequately appreciated. These are the tasks for the future.

Part II

The Solidarity Fund for Economic and Social Development in Non-Aligned Countries—a case study

Reasons for an assessment

The Solidarity Fund for Economic and Social Development in Non-Aligned Countries (referred to hereafter as the Fund) has as yet failed to emerge as an operational instrument. The question can validly be raised as to the reasons which prompt any study of such an institution. The reason simply is that several important features in the Fund proposal make it deserving of further scrutiny.

First, it was a proposal personally made by a distinguished Head of State, the Emir of Kuwait. Kuwait is not only an OPEC country but one of the two or three developing countries controlling substantial financial surpluses. It had a wealth of experience in establishing financial institutions of this kind.

A proposal emanating from such a background cannot easily be paralleled by any other quarter within the G.77.

Second, it is one of the first proposals in the history of the Non-Aligned Movement for institutionalization in any sector. It would be natural to expect such institutionalization initially in the field of finance. It was an expression of the spirit of collective self-reliance at its best.

Third, though the proposal just preceded the increase in the price of oil in 1973, its elaboration and formulation was during the immediate aftermath of the oil price increase and the burgeoning financial surpluses of OPEC countries. It appears to be a major lost opportunity for the Non-Aligned Movement, at least in hindsight.

Fourth, the Fund is not the only proposal for institutionalization which has been slow to progress; there are several others, and for an appreciation of the ways of the Non-Aligned and the G.77 in implementing such proposals, in addition to meeting the mandates of the Caracas decisions, at least one of them deserves a brief assessment so that conclusions can bc drawn for the improved ordering of these matters.

The origin of the Fund proposal

The proposal for the creation of the Fund was made by the Emir of Kuwait, at the Fourth Non-Aligned Summit in Algiers in August 1973, in his speech to the plenary session of Heads of States.

> We believe in the right of developing countries to take part in consultations and decision-making at all economic levels, in order to achieve results which take into account the interests of the developing countries, particularly in regard to reform of the international monetary system and international trade negotiations. We also believe that developing countries have the right to full sovereignty over their national resources, in accordance with their development policy and economic and social progress. The desire of some advanced countries to form new groups to frustrate the hopes and goals of the developing countries does not facilitate international ties but rather causes their deterioration, which hurts the world economy.
>
> Kuwait has not spared its efforts to take a responsible participation in programmes of economic development with fraternal and friendly states. Realizing the need of developing countries for financial institutions, Kuwait has established a number of national and international

> investment institutes and has founded the Kuwait Fund for Arab Development. It has also worked with other Arab countries to set up the Arab Fund for Economic and Social Development.
>
> In view of the successes which these financial institutions have achieved in initiating action for economic and social development, we have proposed the founding of a fund for economic and social development of the nonaligned countries, in which participation would be voluntary and within the framework of bilateral cooperation.[13]

The words of the Emir of Kuwait were followed by the adoption by the Summit of a resolution on the Fund which decided

> To establish an Economic and Social Development Fund for Non-Aligned Countries, open to the participation of all interested non-aligned countries with the following objectives:
>
> a. financing economic and social development projects and participating in development activities in non-aligned countries;
> b. promoting investment in non-aligned countries in co-operation with similar organizations;
> c. providing technical assistance and services in various economic development fields.

The resolution also mandated the appointment of a Committee of Experts 'to work out the rules and regulations of the Fund and determine its capital.[14]

The progress of the proposal

Primarily due to the determination of Kuwait, speedy progress was evident in the early stages. The Co-ordinating Bureau of the Non-Aligned Countries meeting at ministerial level in Algiers in March 1974 worked out the operational details for the meeting of Experts, which it was decided should be representative of the member countries of the Bureau.[15] It is interesting to note at this stage a significant development, as noted in the Report of the Co-ordinating Bureau itself in connection with the Fund. 'The Bureau', says the Report, 'noted with appreciation the decision of the Government of Kuwait to transform the Fund for Arab Economic Development into a fund for the development of all developing countries, and to raise the capital of the Fund from \$600 million to \$3,000 million.' The significance lies in the creation of an institution by Kuwait which could now be a channel to transfer Kuwaiti resources to non-aligned and other developing countries. This development, however, did not affect Kuwait's interest in the

Solidarity Fund in view of the latter's multilateral nature. Its speedy creation would in fact have led to a mutually reinforcing growth and accumulation of experience which of course was to be denied by the course of events.

The economic experts met in Kuwait in May 1974, and worked on the basis of a draft agreement prepared by Kuwait. The task of actual drafting of a legal instrument was left to the legal experts, who met subsequently in January 1975. Of the seventeen governments invited for the meeting of economic experts, twelve countries sent representatives.[16]

Before discussing the substantive content of the Convention establishing the Fund, the steps leading to its adoption and subsequent attrition might be briefly noted. The economic experts submitted an agreed report to the Ministers of Foreign Affairs of Non-Aligned Countries meeting in New York in September 1974, who then referred the report to a Committee of Legal Experts, which met in Kuwait in January 1975.[17] The draft Convention prepared by the legal experts was considered by the Ministerial Meeting of the Co-ordinating Bureau held in Havana in March 1975, and on the basis of its recommendations was finally adopted by the Conference of Ministers of Foreign Affairs of Non-Aligned Countries held in Lima in August 1975. The headquarters of the Fund was to be located in Kuwait. An important point made in the Report of the Havana Co-ordinating Bureau must be noted. It recommended that 'the equal contribution of each member to the Fund's capital be fixed at a level that would not cause undue hardship to the poorer members.'[18] This is a question which will be discussed below.

The Lima Foreign Ministers Conference adopted the Convention and agreed:

> To fix the equal subscription of each member of the Fund at the amount of 500,000 SDR's to be paid in 4 annual instalments in freely convertible currencies, as provided for in Article 7 of the Convention. The totality of these subscriptions will constitute the initial capital of the Fund and will be supplemented, after the establishment of the Fund, by additional voluntary subscriptions as provided for in Article 10 of the Convention.

The Conference expressed the hope that the Fund 'begin its operation before the forthcoming Summit Conference of Non-Aligned Countries to be held in Colombo in August 1976.'[19]

The Statute has been open for signature now for nearly seven years, and only twenty-three countries have either signed, acceded to or ratified it, when compared with the requirement for the Fund's activation fixed at forty member countries. The various conferences of the non-aligned countries since that time have confirmed and called for the early functioning of the Fund, and repeatedly urged the accession of the requisite number of members without success. The members who have signed, acceded to or ratified the Statute are as follows:

> Algeria, Bangladesh, Benin, Cuba, Democratic Korea, Egypt, India, Indonesia, Jamaica, Kuwait, Malaysia, Nepal, Niger, Panama, Peru, Sri Lanka, Sudan, Tanzania, Tunisia, Upper Volta, Vietnam, Yugoslavia and Zaïre.

There is no particular pattern to be discerned in those who are signatories. In 1979, at the Sixth Non-Aligned Summit held in Havana, the Action Programme on Economic Co-operation 'requested the Government of Kuwait, the depositary country of the Agreement, to convene a meeting of plenipotentiaries before December 1979 to review and modify the present Statute, so that the Fund may become operational as soon as possible.' This request was not considered favourably by Kuwait, as it was obvious from the discussions at previous meetings that the object of any modification was Article 60 of the Statute which fixed the minimum number of countries for activating the Fund at forty. Kuwait is not in agreement with any proposal to reduce the minimum.[20] As late as February 1981, in New Delhi at the Conference of Foreign Ministers of Non-Aligned Countries, the request was again repeated for members to accede to the Statute. The Solidarity Fund's present status stands in that indeterminate position.

The Statute of the Fund[21]

The Statute establishing the Fund gives a clear indication of its objectives. The Fund is intended to participate actively in the financing of development projects through direct loans, to promote investment in co-operation with other similar institutions, and to be a source of technical assistance.

Article 12 of the Statute on operating principles is worth quoting as it explains not only the nature of the Fund but also its characteristics which make it distinct from other agencies.

(a) The Fund shall aim at conducting its operations in a manner which serves the interests of all its member countries while paying due regard to the needs of the least developed countries among its members, including land-locked countries and countries suffering from natural disasters.
(b) The Fund shall adopt the recognized principles of development finance on concessionary terms without adversely affecting the soundness of its financial position.
(c) The Fund may complement other available sources of finance to the best interest of its member countries but shall not assist any undertaking able to obtain elsewhere adequate financing and facilities on terms and conditions that the Fund considers reasonable, taking into account all pertinent factors.
(d) Finance shall be provided in terms appropriate to the nature of each operation and to the circumstances of the recipient country. In defining such terms in relation to its activities in the less-developed among its member countries, the Fund shall give due consideration to the situation prevailing in these countries and to their need for softer terms financing.
(e) In providing finance the Fund shall pay due regard to the prospects that the recipient and its guarantor, if any, will be in a position to meet their obligations, but no member country shall be generally excluded from the operations of the Fund merely on the basis of its weak financial position.
(f) Necessary measures shall be taken to ensure that the proceeds of any financing made are used only for the purposes for which it was granted and with due attention to considerations of economy and efficiency.
(g) The proceeds of any financing provided by the Fund shall be used only for procurement in member countries of goods and services produced in such countries to the extent that such goods and services may be procured therein on reasonable terms. Exceptions to this principle may be made in any case in which the Board of Directors determines to allow procurement in a non-member country in special circumstances making such procurement appropriate either in relation to a specific project or in the light of the financial policy of the Fund.

The Fund is to be a concessionary source of finance, and particular emphasis is placed on the provision of finance to the poorer developing countries. An important question that is not fully answered in the situation is the source from which concessionary funds are to be forthcoming, as the mandatory capital of the Fund will be extremely modest at 500,000 SDRs per country.

Article 6 laid down that the resources of the Fund shall consist of:

I The subscribed capital composed initially of equal subscriptions by members;
II Additional voluntary subscriptions by members;
III Other resources received by the Fund from members or non-members;
IV Funds derived from operations or otherwise accruing to the Fund. (Borrowing in capital markets was envisaged once the Fund became operational.)

These provisions appear to be less than definitive with regard to the financial capacity to be generated by the Fund and could be one reason for the hesitant response it has received so far. From the inception of the idea of the Fund, there has been pressure, on the one hand, to make it a source of concessionary aid and, on the other, to make it a viable financial institution controlled by non-aligned countries to generate the required development finance, even on a non-concessional basis. The provisions of the statute did not fully solve the dilemma of these contending claims—the modest sources of financing envisaged being no match to the promises of concessionary finance. The Statute appears to bear a degree of responsibility for the disappointments that were to ensue, though the NAM itself has not looked at this aspect, concentrating merely on obtaining forty signatures. Even if the Fund became operational, it is doubtful on that basis whether it would have become relevant.

Particularly noteworthy features of the Fund were those which addressed themselves to the problems associated with intergovernmental and inter-country co-operation or joint ventures. Assistance from the Fund was to be provided to interregional, regional, and subregional organizations established by member countries for the purpose of serving economic and social development in non-aligned countries. Joint projects between member countries were to be encouraged (Article 14). Technical assistance was to be given in the design and development of these projects and in particular 'technical and financial assistance for the promotion of exports' is mentioned.

The Fund, with these objectives as to the nature of its

assistance, would be in a unique position to promote and establish joint ventures in almost any sector wherever it was economically viable. Producer associations for commodities, multinational marketing enterprises, joint venture projects in agriculture, industry and transport, would all have qualified for financing from the Fund, and it is these ventures that are constantly visualized in repeated Action Programmes of developing countries.[22]

Another distinctive feature was its democratic constitution which ensured one member, one vote on the Board of Governors:

> Additional subscriptions shall form part of the capital of the Fund and shall entitle each contributing member to the number of shares corresponding with the amount of its subscription. Such shares shall not however entitle their bearer to any additional voting rights in the Board of Governors.[23]

There is no doubt again of the laudable intentions of the framers of the Statute. But did this provision weaken the enthusiasm of potential contributing countries? Apart from Kuwait, only two other OPEC members—Algeria and Indonesia—have acceded to the Statute so far. In the International Fund for Agricultural Development, a voting structure was derived which recognized the special role of contribution of capital even within developing countries. It might well be asked whether a similar arrangement would produce an improved response. The statutes of the Islamic Development Bank, alluded to below, are also relevant on this point.[24]

The other remaining critical feature of the Statute, as voted above, is Article 60, which laid down that 'this Convention shall enter into force when instruments of ratification or acceptance have been deposited by at least 40 member countries.' There have been several views as to the feasible minimum number. To obtain even a modest capital structure, a larger minimum number of countries is required, to lower the capital subscription per member. Having decided on 500,000 SDRs per member, forty countries would mean contributions of only 20 million SDRs—an extremely low figure for a development finance institution of this nature. This is another contradiction in the Statute which needs reconsideration. Experience also bears out that though there are over 100 developing countries, the number of countries participating in any one venture is only a fraction of that number. The most successful of developing country projects—the International Centre for Public Enterprises in Ljubljana, Yugoslavia—has no more than forty countries, and some others, like the Centre for International Co-operation to be located in Havana, have failed to evoke an appreciable response. Projects might therefore be designed with smaller numbers in view, at least at the beginning.[25]

What future for the Fund?

The solidarity Fund has developed quite a small head of steam which it would be sad to waste. Not many NAM and G.77 projects have come even this far. It is therefore necessary to consider the feasibility of getting the Fund started, though in a revised form. At the Havana Summit a request was made, as referred to above, to the Government of Kuwait to convene a Conference of Plenipotentiaries to 'review and modify' the Statute. The Government of Kuwait was not in favour as the request was predicated on the revision specifically of Article 60 which fixed the minimum number of countries at forty. With the individual subscription fixed at 500,000 SDRs, the Fund was far too small in size to make it even more insignificant by any revision of only Article 60. However, a more comprehensive revision could be undertaken in the context of developments, since the Fund was initially mooted nearly ten years ago.

At the time the Fund was proposed there were not many multilateral financial agencies specifically designed either for the non-aligned or the developing countries. Since that time, several agencies have emerged to cater to the needs of some of the developing countries. The Islamic Development Bank now has a membership of thirty-four countries and an authorized capital of $2.3 billion. But the Bank does not have a universal membership of either non-aligned or developing countries.

Another major element of the Solidarity Fund which requires revision is its character as a source of concessionary finance and, in particular, its appearance as an aid agency. Non-aligned countries at the time of the drafting of the Statute attempted to shape it more as an aid agency than as a venture in collective self-reliance. The Statute itself has an ambivalence in this regard; though concessionary finance was provided for, there was no specific mechanism through which the cost of such concessions—interest subsidies, for example—were to be met. The general provision for 'voluntary contributions' is the probable mechanism but that lacks certainty and assurance. The capital of the Fund is far too small to generate resources which could meet the cost of subsidies beyond a very modest scale.[26]

The trouble with the Fund solely as a source of concessionary finance in the 1980s is that the picture of OPEC surpluses has changed, and other agencies like the OPEC Fund and IFAD cater for such needs. IFAD has difficulties in assuring replenishment of its resources, and the OPEC Fund has to meet growing demands of the oil-importing developing countries for concessionary finance. Another agency of the same type is not the answer. However, it is important to sustain the commitment of Kuwait—a front-rank financial power in the developing world.

When the Fund was first proposed, it was confined to non-aligned countries and has remained so. However, it may now be relevant to amend this provision so as to enable countries who are members of the G.77 to qualify. The NAM since around 1976 has treated G.77 members as eligible for full participation in any ventures or enterprises urged in the Action Programme on Economic Co-operation of the Non-Aligned Conferences. Such an extension of membership eligibility should bring in several important Latin American countries.

Given the general considerations noted above, three other modifications which should be considered are:

(a) the minimum number of members which now stands at forty;
(b) the capital subscription fixed at 500,000 SDRs per member; and
(c) the one country, one vote principle.

As pointed out above, to obtain the active support of forty member countries of the NAM, let alone the G.77, on any individual project is extremely difficult. This is the experience of the last decade which need not be elaborated here. In the particular case of the Fund, there have also been competing loyalties (the Islamic Development Bank, for instance). It might be relevant to consider a minimum number of twenty countries but on condition that items (b) and (c) above are also modified.

The capital subscription was fixed at such a low figure primarily as a result of the pressures of the poorer and least developed countries, at a time when another source exclusively of concessionary finance was feasible. It is not proposed to do away with that element altogether, as will be described below. However, it is necessary to be realistic about the new demand of the 1980s, wherein financially surplus developing countries seek avenues to channel their surpluses towards remunerative ends and the major gap in development finance requirements of developing countries. For the Fund to be viable in such a context, a capital of at least 100 million SDRs is a minimum and the raising of an individual members' capital to 5 million SDRs should therefore be considered. A minimum of twenty members paying 5 million SDRs should be the point at which the Fund could be activated. The provisions which allow countries to join in on a 500,000 SDR subscription could be maintained but with a voting weight one-tenth of a member country paying the 5 million SDR subscription. The Islamic Development Bank's financial and voting structure is instructive in this context. The main suppliers of finance, Kuwait, Libya, Saudi Arabia and the United Arab Emirates, possess nearly 50 per cent of the voting power. If the Solidarity Fund is to regain credibility and adequate finance, the voting and capital structure must be renegotiated, with more decision-making power to the providers of capital. The above description of 5 million SDRs as a capital subscription is merely a signal for revision, and more dramatic changes might be necessary. The demands made in the early stages of the draft statute to introduce equality of voting power might be a good principle of solidarity, but has weakened considerably the chances of the Fund emerging even as a business proposition.

We come now to the question of concessionary finance. The creation of a distinct interest subsidy account through voluntary contributions must be considered, and some of the developing country donors could agree to long-term commitments to the subsidy account.

The proposals outlined in this section would alter the shape and form of the Fund beyond recognition. The question then arises as to why a new statute should not be considered altogether. As noted at the start, there is a commitment of a country like Kuwait to this Fund and for practical reasons continuity is better than breaking up and starting all over again. The revision of the Statute can take many forms and the proposals made above are only indicative and point us towards new directions. Further study is obviously required for a fresh initiative.

Right from the start, the Fund envisaged the financing of joint ventures and technical assistance. The need for concessionary finance is probably less for joint ventures accepted on the basis of commercial criteria than for development projects at a national level. The technical assistance component of the Fund could well be linked up with the creation of the Project Development Facility[27] which has been mooted independently. If the Fund is redesigned in a manner which emphasizes its potential contribution to joint ventures, a unique role could be carved for it in the present international context. Some tentative observations might be made in the light of the experience of the Fund proposal. The Statute as it stands is a period piece, reflecting the particular international circumstances of the early and middle years of the 1970s. This was a time when a strong spirit of solidarity moved non-aligned and developing countries to self-reliant action. There is a tide in the affairs of men and governments, and the Solidarity Fund for several reasons missed out on that opportunity. Other institutions like the Islamic Development Bank and IFAD came to fruition, and looking at their comparative experience, it might be stated that the very modest volume of the Fund proposal was one of the reasons for its neglect. With a small capital base it never was too attractive to participants, and democracy in voting structures does not go well with financial credibility. The Islamic Development Bank paid due regard to such an imperative. It may also be that a successful venture will have to be started by a like-minded few, and not necessarily await more global participation. Provision should be made for countries to join at a subsequent stage. This is obviously the reason for the greater success of subregional institutions. In institution-building, developing countries also have to bear in mind that costs are involved even for the least developed country, if future gains are to be ensured. Someone has to pay even for the preparation of a report. In the case of the Fund, Kuwait did the preliminary work. Other proposed institutions have languished even without a feasibility report, as there is no mechanism to facilitate the financing of modest levels of technical support. Some machinery to monitor and develop proposals and commitments is an urgent requisite both for the G.77 and NAM.

Notes

1. The G.24 was set up on the basis of a decision at the Second Ministerial Meeting of the G.77 held in Geneva in January 1972. The Chairman of the G.24, in her report to the Third Ministerial Meeting in Manila of the G.77 in 1976, referred to the need 'to re-examine from a political angle the terms of reference initially given to the Group of Twenty-Four in connexion with monetary reform, and to consider the possibility of using the Group as a co-ordinating body with wider terms of reference in the international economic and financial field, including using it as a practical mechanism for strengthening and developing co-operation among the developing countries themselves in those fields.' It is a matter that has still to be pursued. Would it be a satisfactory mechanism if a G.24 were created in Geneva with the identical country membership as the G.24 in Washington to monitor developments in an NIEO context and liaise with the main G.24?
2. A feasible first step is for the NAM or the G.77 to request periodic progress reports from these bodies along with recommendations for further advance in their work. A standing subgroup could monitor developments on the basis of these reports. Incremental improvement of this kind has significant advantages.
3. Final Communiqué, Asian-African Conference, Bandung, April 1955.
4. All references in this paragraph are to the texts of declarations and communiqués issued at the end of these Conferences. Reprinted in Jankowitsch and Sauvant, *The Third World without Superpowers*, Oceana, 1978.
5. See *The Georgetown Declaration, The Action Programme for Economic Co-operation and Related Documents: Conference of Foreign Ministers of Non-Aligned Countries* (Ministry of Foreign Affairs, Georgetown, Guyana, 1972).
6. See Report reprinted in Jankowitsch and Sauvant, op. cit.
7. 'Co-operation in Financial and Monetary Matters among Non-Aligned Countries'. Paper presented by India and Indonesia to the Fourth Conference of Heads of Government or State of Non-Aligned Countries, Algiers, September 1973 (Conference Doc. NAC/ALG/CONF.4/M/C.2/L.12 of 5 September 1973).
8. The Dakar Conference of 1975 represents the peak of developing country self-reliance. Institutions proposed and adopted at the

Conference such as the Common Fund for Buffer Stocks (not the UN but the developing country fund) and the Council of Producer Associations failed to make any headway. There has been no attempt to undertake a comprehensive revision of the strategy for primary commodities in the wake of these failures.

9. See Report of the Representatives of the Co-ordinator Countries on Financial and Monetary Co-operation, Belgrade, 30 June–2 July 1977.
10. See the Proceedings of the Conference of Foreign Ministers of Non-Aligned Countries held in New Delhi in February 1981. The section on Review of Implementation of the Action Programme for Economic Co-operation under sub-section E on Monetary–Financial co-operation states: 'The Ministers recalled the decision taken at the meeting of the Non-Aligned Co-ordinating Countries held at Belgrade in June–July 1977 and the assertions made at subsequent meetings of the developing countries regarding the need for financial and monetary co-operation by the developing countries. They noted with deep concern the lack of progress made on the five studies on financial and monetary co-operation proposed at the Belgrade Meeting. They urged the group of countries concerned to prepare a time-bound programme so that the Co-ordinating Bureau could take steps to have the studies completed by the end of the year 1981.' With the end of 1981 came the inevitable disappointment, due to the organizational weakness for carrying out this type of assignment.
11. See '1980 Review—Development Co-operation' (OECD).
12. There is a marked ECDC component in the recent batch of studies from UNCTAD on commodity processing and marketing.
13. Proceedings of the Non-Aligned Summit in Algiers, *Review of International Affairs*, Vol. XXIV, No. 564, 5 October 1974 (Belgrade). It is pertinent to observe that the Emir in his speech also called 'for the setting up of a permanent commission for economic affairs of the non-aligned countries which would be a co-ordinating body.'
14. Resolution No. 4 of the Fourth Summit of Non-Aligned Countries on the Establishment of the Economic and Social Development Fund for Non-Aligned Countries.
15. See the Report of the Co-ordinating Bureau of Non-Aligned Countries, Algiers, March 1974.
16. The countries invited were Algeria, Cuba, India, Jamaica, Kuwait, Sri Lanka, Liberia, Mali, Malaysia, Nepal, Peru, Syria, Senegal, Somalia, Tanzania, Yugoslavia and Zaïre. Liberia, Malaysia, Senegal, Somalia and Tanzania were not represented at the meeting. Yugoslavia presented a paper on the proposed Fund which was made use of by the experts in their work, in addition to the Kuwait draft.
17. The Committee of Economic Experts was chaired by Mr Abdlatif Y. Al-Hamad, presently Minister of Finance of Kuwait, and the Secretary

of the Committee was Dr Ibrahim F. I. Shihata. Dr Shihata subsequently chaired the Committee of Legal Experts. Dr Shihata is now the Secretary-General of the OPEC Fund in Vienna.

18. See the Declaration of the Meeting of the Co-ordinating Bureau, at Ministerial Level, held in Havana in March 1975.
19. See resolution X: Establishment of the Solidarity Fund for Economic and Social Development in the Non-Aligned Countries and Annex containing Convention establishing the Solidarity Fund for Economic and Social Development in Non-Aligned Countries, Conference of Ministers for Foreign Affairs of Non-Aligned Countries, Lima, August 1975.
20. Information obtained on the basis of personal interviews.
21. The State or Convention of the Fund referred to hereafter in this chapter is the text adopted at Lima in 1975. It was opened for signature in New York in October 1975 and Kuwait was the first signatory. The statute still remains open for accession at the Ministry of Foriegn Affairs, Kuwait.
22. The feasibility of financing developing country joint venture projects could in fact be the focal orientation in any future project.
23. This was an excellent expression of the spirit of collective self-reliance. It was probably too far ahead of the times to come. Developing countries with a financial surplus would have found themselves contributing to a Fund over which they have no control.
24. Both these institutions date back to the identical period as the Fund, and come, more or less, from the same stable. It is therefore interesting to see why they managed to evolve into viable financial institutions while the Fund did not. Even poorer developing countries made substantial contributions to IFAD voluntarily (e.g., Sri Lanka US $1 million). The size of the contribution, though much emphasis was placed on it by member countries, is not the key to greater participation.
25. NAM and G.77 must consider this aspect more carefully. The viability of a project proposal does not depend so much on numbers as on its economic rationale. A minimum critical number and, within that number, the quality and the determination of participants are important. But how many? It could even be four or five for most projects and not necessarily confined to a region. Like-mindedness is significant even with an organization like NAM.
26. It could be argued that the very features of equal contributions and equal votes makes the Fund anything but an aid agency. But with that level of contributions, the Fund would have been inactive, if voluntary contributions were not forthcoming purely in a spirit of solidarity. The concept of solidarity and the demands of real world finance, it is felt, were not satisfactorily resolved within the Statute.

27. Project Development Facility, which has been a NAM project on the drawing board for the last decade is more amenable as a subsidiary or Department of the Fund; a similar arrangement was visualized for PDF in the context of the Commercial and Merchant Bank for developing countries.

3 REVIEW OF PROPOSALS FOR THIRD WORLD FINANCIAL CO-OPERATION

R. STAMENKOVIĆ

Introduction

1. During the two preceding decades, financial and monetary co-operation has emerged as an important component of economic co-operation among developing countries. As in some other forms, co-operation in this particular area has progressed fastest within the orbits of the various economic groupings. The formation of subregional and regional clearing arrangements has been among the earliest forms of such co-operation. Some of these arrangements came to be complemented with credit institutions aimed at stimulating mutual trade and, in most cases, providing support to the global payments balances of the member countries. Some more advanced groupings have also succeeded in setting up export credit facilities.

2. In the area of development finance, the co-operative efforts of developing countries have resulted in the creation of subregional development institutions like those in the Caribbean, Central America and the Andean subregion. These efforts have also been at the base of the international co-operation which has resulted in the establishment of the regional development banks. In the course of the 1970s, a new important source of development finance emerged in the form of development funds and institutions established collectively, or individually by the oil-exporting countries, members of OPEC. Net financial flows from this new source amounted to US $5.2 billion, with concessional flows accounting for about 60 per cent of the total. An important feature of policies relating to the transfer of resources from OPEC member countries to other developing countries has been the emergence of joint ventures located in the capital-importing countries and serving the mutual interests of the parties involved.

3. However, in the light of the present world economic situation and of the prospects ahead, the past achievements of developing countries appear comparatively modest. The deterioration of the external payments position of most developing countries in recent years has imposed painful adjustments, invariably at the expense of growth and other development objectives. With no amelioration of the world situation in sight, developing countries would have to rely much more on their own forces, even on the assumption that aid from developing countries would tangibly increase in the coming years. Collective self-reliance came to be recognized as a particularly promising avenue to development and progress. However, the success of collective self-reliance seems to depend above all on a higher degree of Third World solidarity in the financial area.

4. A move towards a closer monetary and financial co-operation has been observable of late. Actually, as witnessed by the efforts of economic groupings, there is a pronounced tendency to improve and widen the networks of subregional and regional financial facilities and to provide support to the establishment of similar facilities elsewhere. Parallel to this, attempts are being made to devise arrangements and mechanisms which transgress the boundaries of individual groupings and pave the way to co-operation at the Third World level. As will be seen, the proposals reviewed in sections II and III of the present report aim at accelerating the co-operation movement in both directions.

5. While the efforts of developing countries along the lines above may be expected to produce some results, the progress of the Third World towards establishing its own financial base will essentially depend on the orientation of the aid, financial and investment policies of the surplus OPEC countries. It is therefore important to note that some of the proposals related to development finance reviewed in section I of this report, come precisely from OPEC sources. These proposals reflect a clear perception of the common interest of the OPEC members and of other developing countries in establishing mutually beneficial forms of co-operation. As described in a study from a prominent author,[1] direct co-operation between the Arab oil-producing countries and other developing countries should be regarded as a means for promoting economic development throughout

these two groups of countries alike. It should lead to greater specialization, increased transfer of resources and expanding investment opportunities. The underlying objective of such co-operation should be the establishment of a system of economic relations that would yield mutual and lasting benefits to both parties. The goal of such co-operation should be the improvement of living standards in the developing countries and, in the longer run, the attainment of self-sustaining growth for all countries concerned. In view of the envisioned interdependence and the close co-operation required to realize these objectives, Arab oil-producing countries and the other countries of the Third World can be rightly regarded as true 'Partners in Development'.

6. The present report consists of the following sections:

I Development Finance
II Export Finance
III Payments Arrangements and Reserve Funds.

It should be added that while the major official proposals have been relatively easy to trace, it has been very difficult to do so with proposals and suggestions coming from unofficial sources. Some of the latter might have been omitted in the report, particularly if contained in publications which are not easily available.

I Development finance

1. In the course of the last three to four years, several proposals have been made by developing countries, all aiming at increasing the flows of development resources and improving the existing mechanisms of international finance. Some of these proposals rely exclusively on increased flows from developed countries,[2] others on combined contributions from OPEC sources and developed countries. Only one proposal aims at the establishment of a true Third World development agency, based on a high degree of solidarity between the financially strong and the poor members of the Third World community.

2. In the subsequent paragraphs two governmental proposals will be reviewed first: the proposal by Iraq made in 1979, and

then the joint proposal by Algeria and Venezuela, put forward towards the end of the same year. In addition, two unofficial proposals, coming from private quarters, will be examined. The first concerns the establishment of a global investment trust; the second contemplates certain forms of co-operation which might induce private capital in Arab countries to engage in ventures located in other developing regions, sub-Saharan Africa in particular. Following this, a couple of proposals concerning pre-investment facilities, a proposal for the establishment of a Third World bank, and a few proposals concerning energy will be briefly reviewed.

A. The Iraqi proposal[3]

3. In 1979, the Government of Iraq proposed the establishment of a new international institution—an international fund—largely conceived as an instrument for compensating the oil-importing developing countries for the losses incurred through the continued rise in import prices. The contributions to the fund's resources—from members of OPEC and from developed countries—would be determined automatically. The first group of countries would contribute annually amounts corresponding to the losses of non-oil producing countries, caused by increases in the price of crude oil imported for domestic consumption. Similarly, the contribution of the second group would be determined by the rise in prices (relative to a selected base year) of its export goods imported by the non-oil countries.[4] The fund should have a lifetime of not less than ten years and its assistance would be mainly in the form of grants, at least in the initial stage of operations.

4. The main merit of the Iraqi proposal lies in the fact that it draws attention to the plight of the non-oil developing countries exposed to the mounting pressure of inflation coming from two different sources: price increases in products imported from the developed countries and the rise in oil prices. Furthermore, the automaticity of the proposed system would be an advantage from the point of view of the potential beneficiaries. However, as long as the compensation to be provided by the oil-exporting countries remained tied to the corresponding compensation by the developed countries, the establishment of the proposed institution would remain beyond the control of the Third World.

B. *Algerian–Venezuelan proposal: an agency for development and economic co-operation among developing countries*[5]

5. As proposed by the two governments, the OPEC Special Fund should be converted into a development agency, with its own international legal personality, which would function as an intergovernmental institution. It would finance its activities through its own resources and through the sale of financial instruments in the international financial markets. All developing countries should be able to become beneficiaries, taking into account their specific situation;in particular, the conditions of financing should be suited to the general economic situation of individual countries, the degree of dependence on imported energy and the balance of payments position. In the distribution of aid, priority will be given to the least developed and the most seriously affected countries, each of which should enjoy special conditions. The agency would grant loans for specific projects capable of yielding an adequate rate of return on capital, as well as concessional loans in accordance with the needs and situation of individual countries.

6. The agency's activities would cover the following areas:

- (i) financing of balance of payments deficits;
- (ii) financing under favourable terms of economic and social development projects recognized by the recipient countries as priority projects, including the development of renewable and non-renewable sources of energy;
- (iii) financing of projects intended to reinforce integration between developing countries in order to promote their collective self-reliance;
- (iv) financing of projects intended to upgrade the value of the raw materials produced by developing countries;
- (v) underwriting of export credit between developing countries, especially in the area of energy supply;
- (vi) financing of commercial operations of developing countries under market conditions;
- (vii) underwriting loans floated by developing countries on financial loans;
- (viii) promotion of procurement of goods and services available in member countries in the context of the agency's loan policies.

7. The authorized capital of the agency is set at US $20 billion (200,000 shares at $100,000 each), with the possibility of further periodic increases, the modalities of which remain to be worked out. Half of the total capital would be paid in and the other half callable. The paid-in part would consist of:

(i) the $4 billion assets of the OPEC Special Fund;[6]
(ii) $1 billion to be paid in at the outset by the founding OPEC members;
(iii) $5 billion cash payments by either OPEC or other developing countries, according to a three-year schedule.

The developing countries' debtors to the OPEC Special Fund could acquire shares by settling their outstanding obligations towards the latter. In order to mobilize additional resources, bonds would be sold on international markets, with the expectation that the founding members would be the first purchasers. Each country member of the agency would have a number of votes according to its number of shares, and the major decisions would be taken by a qualified majority.

8. A number of features of the proposed agency, such as its organization *modus operandi*, assistance criterion, the precise way in which individual activities would be carried out, etc., would have to be worked out in greater detail. Moreover, from what is known it would seem that the proposal has been under intensive discussion for some time in the competent OPEC bodies, the outcome of which have not been made public yet. Under the circumstances it would be too early to attempt a close scrutiny of the proposed agency. The few comments which will be made below are of a more general nature and they occasionally go a little beyond what is actually contained in the proposal.

9. First of all, it should be pointed out that the proposal by Algeria and Venezuela reflects a clear perception of the leading role which the OPEC countries could assume in the promotion of solidarity of the Third World. In the words of the sponsors of the agency:

> Its great advantage would consist in the fact that the financial resources of the OPEC member countries could be used to augment significantly

the amount of aid extended to other developing countries. At the same time, the participation in the agency by other developing countries could eventually lead to a shared responsibility on the question of development assistance and, consequently, release pressure on the OPEC countries.

10. At the present juncture, with difficulties and problems crowding from all points, the emergence of an important source of finance from the Third World itself would be likely to provide a much-needed boost to the self-confidence of developing countries, which is essential for the success of collective self-reliance. A development agency of an adequate size could indeed become the main support of the Third World co-operation. Furthermore, the more permanent forms of co-operation and co-ordination which such a body could establish with other international institutions might be expected to make the whole mechanism of international finance more effective and better adapted to the Third World's needs.

11. Clearly, it would not be realistic to expect that the proposed agency could meet all the immediate needs of the developing countries. If a 'more permanent mechanism of financial co-operation' is to be established, attention must be given to its viability, and it would be up to the developing countries to watch this. From what can be gathered the sponsors of the agency propose a careful approach. The proportion of resources to be devoted to concessional finance is not indicated, but the impression is that this type of finance would be reserved for the most needy countries. On the other hand, the sponsors seem to attach great importance to profit-yielding activities, which, under the circumstances, seems understandable. It is obvious that the viability of the institution would largely depend on its attractiveness to subscribers and lenders, and hence on its capacity to guarantee competitive returns on capital. A clear demarcation line therefore would have to be drawn between the concessional and non-concessional activities, and their relative priorities should be determined in the light of realistically assessed possibilities.

12. Although many details concerning the forms and scope of activities of the proposed body are not available at this stage, it

would seem that the predominant part of the resources would be directed to sectors and projects which contribute most to the diversification, integration and overall strength of the economic base of the Third World. Assistance, therefore, would probably concentrate on large and promising projects in such areas as energy and mineral resources, transport facilities, agriculture and related industries.

13. It might be expected that, in addition to direct assistance, a development agency of the type proposed could play a crucial role in the promotion of long-term investments, joint ventures and various forms of multinational undertakings which, when necessary, might be complemented by suitable forms of co-operation with firms and institutions from developed countries, particularly where advanced technology and technical skills are needed. It is often pointed out that joint ventures between OPEC countries and other developing countries especially could play an important role in the development of the Third World economy as the interests of the two groups converge.[7] Many developing countries which have a large resource base but not the means to put it under exploitation are unwilling to accept the terms of transnationals or other potential investors from the industrialized world. Many OPEC countries, on the other hand, largely depend on a single and exhaustible resource; to ensure reliable sources of supply and protect their economies against inflation imported from industrialized countries, they will increasingly have to look for promising investment within their own world. Clearly, the success of the promotional role of the proposed agency would greatly depend on its ability to set up—in co-operation with regional and national institutions—highly efficient services for identifying promising projects and carrying out pre-investment work.

14. Depending on the size of available resources, there are many ways not listed among the proposed activities in which a development agency could promote collective self-reliance and provide support to the developing countries in their relations with the industrialized ones.

(i) As already suggested above, the position of Third World host countries when negotiating terms and conditions with foreign investors from the developed countries would be considerably stronger if they could count on an alternative source of finance.

(ii) In the critical area of balance of payments finance, developing countries are in the process of developing special forms of co-operation, largely through efforts to set up mutual support schemes among the existing subregional credit arrangements. Assistance from a development institution, possibly in the form of subsidized loans, could do much to reinforce and expand the envisaged schemes, which might ultimately encompass the entire Third World.

(iii) In the no less critical area of export finance, relatively modest contributions could help developing countries to set up an international guarantee facility and/or open new regional sources of export finance.

(iv) In the commodity area, the least that a development agency could do would be to promote and assist producers' associations, but it could go further and take the initiative for setting up effective commodity stabilization arrangements which would greatly improve the position of developing countries *vis-à-vis* the industrialized world.

(v) Furthermore, the close ties which should normally develop between a central body and regional development banks and agencies, would strengthen the position of the latter and would contribute to the formulation of a coherent set of financial and development policies, well adapted to the real national and collective needs of Third World countries.

15. The proposed capital of the agency seems amply sufficient for starting the operations, but it does not seem too large in comparison with the surpluses which the OPEC member states may expect in the coming years. According to World Bank estimates, if the percentage of the GNP of OPEC member countries going to development assistance continues at the present level, around $10 billion would be available in 1985 and some $15 billion in 1990. A reasonable portion of this assistance flow could ensure a smooth functioning of the agency's soft window.

16. It may be important to note that if a correct balance were found between the concessional and non-concessional activities, and if the latter were efficiently run, the lending risks involved

should not be particularly high—at least not higher than in the case of most other investments. If the alternative were the placement of deposits in the banks of developed countries, the risks would not differ much as many of these banks are heavily involved in foreign lending. In 1977, for instance, as much as two-thirds and four-fifths of the total profits of the two leading New York banks consisted of foreign earnings. The non-oil developing countries which expect large financial and energy resources from OPEC member countries, and would assume part of the responsibility for the state of the agency, would be likely to give full attention to the servicing of their debt.

17. It might be remarked at the end that, compared with the actual practice of international financial institutions, the proposed 50 per cent ratio of the paid-in to total capital appears excessively high. The World Bank started with a 20 per cent ratio; this was reduced to 10 per cent in the course of the first capital increase, and is expected to go down to 7.5 per cent in the current increase. The same amount of cash contribution to the agency's capital as envisaged in the proposal could probably safely support a considerably larger capital and, hence, a considerably larger volume of activities.

C. A global investment trust (GIT)[8]

18. The proposed GIT is conceived as an independent semi-public institution with an authorized capital of SDR 20 billion (with a paid-in part of SDR 5 billion), and with equal participation for three groups of countries—OPEC, non-OPEC developing and developed countries. The contributions to the paid-in part of capital would not have to be made entirely in approved foreign currencies. Part could also be made in the form of commitments to deliver specified types of goods and services. Besides, to make it easier for poorer developing countries, subscriptions could be made by transferring to GIT entitlements to claims on already approved projects. The capital would be held by public institutions or, if so desired, by private or mixed enterprises. Additional resources would be obtained by borrowing from the public and/or the private sector. GIT would only engage in promising ventures, on the important condition that no project would be eligible unless ranking high

on the priority list of the host country. More generally, the interests of the host country would be fully respected.

19. The proposal has been presented in a somewhat sketchy form so that a number of points would have to be clarified or worked out in more precise terms. Even so, the flexibility of the scheme and the underlying views on the roles which a development agency should play deserve attention. According to the author, development financing should not be limited to the traditional role of providing funds but should also focus on the identification and launching of, and operational assistance to, new, economically viable projects. Aware of the difficulty of the task, the author constantly emphasizes the importance of close co-operation between the proposed Trust and the existing international financial institutions, regional and national development agencies, etc. There is a variety of forms in which GIT could offer assistance. Resources could be channelled to the approved projects through loans granted to national or regional development agencies. Alternatively, GIT could engage its own resources, mobilize the necessary services and take full responsibility for the implementation of a project until the take-off stage were reached, then withdraw its capital and invest it elsewhere. Furthermore, GIT could resort to the whole gamut of co-financing and co-management arrangements, with both public agencies and with private institutions and enterprises. Finally, the Trust could limit its role to the identification of promising ventures (in co-operation with competent regional and national agencies) and then, using its promotional facilities and acting as guarantor, bring in capital, technical knowledge and management skill from entirely different sources.

20. As it appears, GIT is conceived as a flexible, semi-private concern whose activities would be run along efficient commercial lines. This, of course, would leave little room for concessional financing.[9] But as the proposal primarily counts on the financial interest of lenders, financiers and entrepreneurs, no alternative course would seem possible. The scheme is, however, seen only as one addition to the international structure of development finance, and not as a substitute for what already exists or what may come into existence.

D. Possible forms of co-operation between Arab countries and other developing countries

21. Certain features reminiscent of those contained in the GIT proposal may be found in a few studies which explore the possibilities of encouraging the flow of private Arab capital to developing countries, notably to sub-Saharan Africa, which is considered a particularly promising region. It is pointed out that, contrary to their behaviour in the initial phase of oil price increases, Arab investors take a growing interest in the control and management of their assets. Moreover, with the often disappointing experience with purely financial investment, preference tends to be given to investments in real assets. So far, Arab investors have been primarily looking for investment opportunities in developed countries, but as it now appears, prospects for continuing to do so are not particularly bright as restrictions imposed on Arab ownership over a range of real assets tend to multiply. As put by an author, 'Arab investors deem the investment climate unfavourable to them.'[10] All this together has tended to enhance of late the interest of Arab capital in promising ventures in developing countries. However, the well-known constraints in both the Arab countries and the prospective host countries, associated with institutional weaknesses, lack of enterpreneurship, technical expertise and know-how, together with the possible risks to which investors would be exposed, continue to present formidable obstacles. There is a wide consensus, therefore, that it would be difficult to envisage a major move on the part of private investors unless associated with strong support and initiative coming from public development and financial institutions of the Arab countries.

22. The points made above are well developed in a recent study which, among other things, suggests the establishment of a *multilateral Arab investment company for sub-Saharan Africa.*[11] Initially, it is said, there would be need for considerable commitments on the part of Arab governments in order to overcome the reluctance of private investors to engage in a hitherto unfamiliar region of investment opportunities; and the private companies to which participation would be extended would be unwilling to accept the risks and administrative

difficulties of investing in Africa. Promotion of investment opportunities by private companies alone would require heavy guarantees covering such risks as nationalization and confiscation, transferability of dividends and principal, and losses caused by war or internal disturbances.

23. The study is very much in favour of joint ventures between Arab investors and appropriate institutions in other developing countries, but attention is drawn to the often-raised issue concerning the difficulty of many host countries to supply acceptable contributions. Besides, in view of the constraints mentioned earlier, joint ventures in most cases would have to be complemented with appropriate forms of co-operation with firms and institutions of developed countries.

24. As in the GIT proposal, the difficulties involved in identifying and evaluating alternative investment projects, particularly where commercial investment is concerned, are seen as a major bottleneck. This, as stated in the study, suggests the need for increased emphasis on the operations of development finance institutions in individual countries. These national development agencies could co-ordinate lines of credit from regional, international and other institutions, and identify and finance projects in line with national development goals. Extending Arab aid through such institutions could be important in relieving the donors of much of the burden of administering aid. Aid channelled through such development banks and agencies could take a range of forms, such as equity participation, the provision of long-term credit lines, the provision of trust funds for specified uses, or co-financing in various forms.

25. While the enormous agricultural potential of Africa seems to be seen as the most promising area for large-scale ventures involving Arab funds, possibilities in other areas—notably energy and mineral resources—have been reviewed too. It is believed that the Arab surplus countries could help not only with the financing of mineral and oil exploration and development, but also in the establishment of processing facilities. Given the potential profitability of such activities, the financial flows could take the form of commercial investments, given appropriate legal safeguards for foreign investments. Moreover,

in the exploration and development of oil and gas resources, private and national Arab companies might be able to provide the required technical expertise.

26. Another important form of co-operation suggested in the study would be the assistance which Arab institutions could provide to African countries for borrowing in international capital markets. Some countries which have been unable to tap commercial sources of credit would be in a much easier position to do so, given Arab sponsorship of their bond issues. This possibility assumes added relevance with the growing willingness of Arab investment funds and banks to act as managers and co-managers for major loans in the Euro-currency markets. The commitment of a limited amount of Arab funds could serve as a catalyst for increasing the flow of commercial credits to African countries.

E. Pre-investment facilities

27. The lack of adequate pre-investment facilities in the Third World continues to present a major obstacle to a wider mobilization and effective channelling of existing resources. As put in a more recent proposal, 'one of the first steps to be taken in the promotion of co-operation among developing countries would be to establish and keep up to date an inventory of possible multinational projects of particular interest to individual regions.'[12] The author of the proposal urges the establishment of close and permanent forms of co-operation among regional and subregional development banks and agencies, and the setting-up of one or more *data banks*, with the support of UNCTAD and UNDP. The author points in particular to the need for identifying and preparing multinational projects and programmes of regional and interregional significance such as, for instance, a vast programme for developing agricultural resources, which would involve the Arab countries and a large number of developing countries in different regions of the world. In this connection, the establishment of a Third World fund (or funds) is suggested. Such a pre-investment institution (or institutions) should identify projects and programmes of the type mentioned, and conduct all the pre-investment work so as to make them operational.

28. It should be recalled, however, that a proposal for the

establishment of a project development facility for developing countries was put forward by India at several conferences of Non-Aligned Countries, starting with the 1973 Algiers Summit. After being adopted at the Colombo Conference, the proposal was submitted to the Foreign Ministers Conference in New Delhi in April 1977, where it was decided that it should be submitted to a group of experts. The proposed facility would operate through the following services: (i) training, surveys, including market and resource surveys, and regional planning studies; (ii) project identification, preparation of pre-feasibility and feasibility studies; (iii) project engineering and design, design of civil works, project construction, procurement, and inspection of equipment; (iv) project implementation and evaluation, modernization studies, capacity utilization, product upgrading studies, project management services, etc.

29. It might be of some interest to mention in this context the newly established and rather modest Caribbean Project Development Facility (CPDF), as it could perhaps serve as an example to a group of countries wishing to establish something similar. Funded by grants from development agencies and international institutions, it should provide pre-project technical assistance to the countries of the region. The central purpose of this small institution is to increase the supply of investment projects worthy of financing and make them known to prospective investors and lenders within and outside the region, including private companies, public and semi-public institutions. For projects in the range of some US $500,000 to $5 million or above, CPDF will generally directly provide advice on a wide number of relevant issues, such as all financial matters concerning a project, staff requirements, sources of necessary supplies, prospective markets, etc. In other cases, CPDF will act as a clearing-house, helping local sponsors to establish contact with domestic or foreign sources capable of carrying out the project preparation work.

F. A banking facility for the Third World

30. Following a proposal made by the Prime Minister of Sri Lanka at the Fifth Non-Aligned Summit in Colombo, and a subsequent resolution on the establishment of a bank of

developing countries, a study bearing the same title was produced on the subject.[13]

31. As seen by the author, the proposed bank would not be a development financial institution but rather a commercial and merchant bank which could engage in virtually all kinds of banking activities, so as to be able to offer a very wide range of services to its potential clients. However, in addition to such activities as operations related to savings and time deposits, current accounts, rediscounting of commercial papers, etc., the bank would particularly engage in (i) the training of banking staff along lines of modern banking techniques; (ii) commercial intelligence of particular interest in trade among developing countries; (iii) marketing research, especially for such products and commodities for which these facilities are lacking; and (iv) identification, evaluation and formulation of projects, including feasibility studies, in agriculture, manufacturing and other sectors. According to the study, the start should be modest—an initial capital of some US $350 million is tentatively envisaged—so that the bank could be established even without special contributions from OPEC sources, and membership would consist of the governments of developing countries only. However, the author expects that such an institution could slowly and gradually establish a network of subsidiaries throughout the Third World, thus taking over an ever increasing part of the ground presently covered by big banking corporations of industrialized countries.

32. It should be added that, according to the author, the rationale for a commercial and merchant bank lies in the historically important role of such institutions in world economic development and the most important role in economic intermediation at the current time. The lack of such banking facilities among developing countries has enabled developed countries' banks to create a virtual monopoly in these skills. It is only institutions of this nature, acting on commercial criteria, which could provide the day-to-day institutional support for transactions of a varied nature encompassed within the framework of ECDC.

G. Energy development

33. The Expert Group, organized under the auspices of the North–South Roundtable in preparation for the UN Conference on New and Renewable Sources of Energy,[14] has proposed the establishment of a new energy investment bank by OPEC, OECD and other countries. Other proposals put forward by the Group related to: (i) increasing the lending capacity of the IBRD by changing its conservative capital-lending ratio; (ii) augmenting the resources and contributions to energy investment of the regional development banks; (iii) investments by innovative corporations combining public with private capital; (iv) establishment of energy affiliates by consortia of commercial banks; (v) establishing guarantee schemes which could help to mobilize additional private capital for energy investments; (vi) other possible innovations such as energy tax, guaranteed energy bonds using surplus OPEC capital, and a Third Window of the World Bank, providing loans with subsidized interest rates to intermediate-level developing countries; and (vii) the establishment of a consultative Group on Energy Investment which would draw together major lenders and development assistance donors from all sectors to consider needs and mobilize the capital and technical resources required to meet them.

34. At the UN Conference on New and Renewable Sources of Energy a proposal was made by the Prime Minister of Jamaica for the estabishment of a specific institution, necessary for accelerating alternative energy technologies.

II Export finance

35. Apart from a short summary of the features of the proposed International Export Credit Guarantee Facility (IECGF), on which work within UNCTAD is going on, three more recent proposals in the export finance area have been selected for examination. The first proposal, or rather a suggestion coming from academic circles, concerns a possible variant of an international guarantee facility for developing countries. The second proposal, put forward in a report submitted to the Committee on ECDC, lays emphasis on the role of the regional export credit insurance facilities and their mutual co-operation.

The third, coming from the same author, concerns the establishment of a foreign trade bank of developing countries which, among other functions, could provide a new source of export finance. In addition to these proposals, the main features of the proposed ACP bank will be briefly summarized.

H. The proposed IECGF

36. The proposed Facility has been under discussion for several years now, but there has been little progress towards its establishment, largely because of the reticence of industrial countries. The technical aspects of the proposal had been explored within UNCTAD through consultations with governmental experts, experts in capital markets as well as with regional, subregional and international financial institutions. Private financial institutions which had been consulted on the subject agreed that paper guaranteed by the Facility would represent an attractive form of financial assets and that the guarantee would improve the discount rates applied. Furthermore, there has been a wide consensus that finance provided by capital markets on guaranteed paper presented for refinancing by the exporting developing countries would be only partially counted within borrowing limits so that there would be substantial additionality in the financial resources available to those countries.

37. The meeting of the Intergovernmental Group of Experts, held in January 1982, has ended up by recommending further study of a few specific features of the proposal. However, progress has been made in defining more precisely the basic features and operations of the proposed Facilities. These have been summarized by the Chairman of the Group of Experts in the following way:

(i) The Facility would guarantee negotiable export credit paper arising from exports of developing countries, normally requiring medium- to long-term credits. The guarantee should represent an unconditional obligation of the Facility to pay the holder of the paper the amount due if drawee or the acceptor fail to honour it at maturity. On its part, the national agency of the exporting country, designated by the government, should unconditionally guarantee to reimburse the Facility on recourse.

(ii) The evaluation of creditworthiness of individual transactions, which have to conform to accepted international norms, should be carried out by the national agency and the Facility. The latter should be empowered to impose limits—by country, exporter, importer or any other basis—whenever sound management of the Facility's resources so required.

(iii) The Facility should have an adequate capital base (in convertible currencies) and be empowered to borrow short-term funds in international capital markets. Its income should derive from the fees paid for the provisions of guarantees and from its investments. The basis for charging fees should reflect the objective of making of the Facility, as early as possible, a self-financing institution.

(iv) The users of the Facility would be developing countries. The membership, however, should be as broad as possible, including intergovernmental financial organizations.[15]

I A guarantee/insurance facility

38. In a recent study[16] which considers various possibilities for attenuating the export credit problems of developing countries, distinction is made between an international facility limited to providing guarantees and a combined guarantee/insurance facility. In the latter case, the international facility might have to bear more substantial risks of possible capital losses, depending on the number of co-insurers and the type of risks for which the insurance cover is provided. The portfolio of export credits should be diversified so that the average risks are minimized. Moreover, the capital requirements for such a Facility would be larger than those for establishing a pure guarantee facility. None the less, according to the study, the second solution would offer considerable advantages to developing countries. First, if there is an insurance cover by an international facility for an export credit instrument of a developing country, its acceptability in the international capital market would significantly improve, thereby reducing the cost of refinance. Secondly, only insurance cover against certain risks, largely of a political nature, would eliminate such risks for the institution providing refinance.

J. Strengthening the existing insurance institutions and their mutual co-operation[17]

39. The formulation of the proposal is preceded by a comprehensive analysis of the performance of the existing regional and subregional export credit insurance mechanisms, notably those in Latin America. Co-operation among these mechanisms could ultimately lead to the creation of a Third World insurance mechanism, but the author is in favour of a gradual approach, which would include the following steps:

(i) organization of meetings of experts of existing institutions, which would examine the possibility of greater co-ordination among them—especially in the diversification of risks—and investigate practical co-insurance and reinsurance formulae;
(ii) promotion of co-operation arrangements at regional and subregional levels whereby countries not operating an insurance scheme might have access to schemes existing elsewhere. These arrangements, which would start by ensuring better and more widespread information concerning such schemes, could be instituted by the regional economic commissions and/or institutions representing the financial interests of countries of a region, notably the regional development banks and foreign trade banks;
(iii) a further step would be for the national and regional institutions to join efforts to set up an insurance facility for developing countries.

40. To make it clear what the regional schemes should do, the author refers to the conclusions of an ESCAP meeting which defines their functions as follows: (i) extending export insurance to countries lacking a national export credit insurance facility; (ii) providing reinsurance facilities for export credits insured by national institutions; (iii) supplying information on the situation and prospects of markets; (iv) providing technical and managerial assistance to countries of the region wishing to establish and develop their national insurance schemes.

41. Another point contained in the proposal concerns exports of capital goods. Referring to the experience of the Inter-American Development Bank, which has set up a special line of

credit for the refinancing of exports of capital goods from the member countries, the author suggests the introduction of a similar facility by the Asian Development Bank, the African Development Bank and by other regional development institutions. The author also points to the desirability of special credit programmes for interregional exports of capital goods, which could be established with lines of credit provided by the regional banks, with some financial support from OPEC.

K. A foreign trade bank for developing countries[18]

42. The author of the preceding proposal also advocates the establishment of a Third World foreign trade bank as an instrument for promoting co-operation among developing countries. For the purpose of financing and promoting trade, a bank, it is said, would be preferable to a fund because of its access to capital markets and its greater ability to mobilize available liquidity, particularly in oil-exporting countries.

43. The main functions of the proposed bank would be:

(i) to support and strengthen existing regional institutions which, through action in the commercial and financial fields, promote trade among developing countries;
(ii) to support, strengthen and promote the establishment of regional export finance and credit insurance institutions for trade among developing countries;
(iii) to support and promote the establishment of auxiliary mechanisms to stimulate trade, such as payments agreements, multinational commodity purchasing enterprises, marketing enterprises, trade information organizations, etc.;
(iv) to finance exports among developing countries, mainly for capital goods, other manufactures, and foodstuffs under special programmes.

The Bank would be an intergovernmental financial institution of second instance, i.e. supporting the action of the national export credit organizations. However, in those countries where there is no governmental body or private financial organization supported by the state to finance export transactions, the bank could perform these operations directly, or else use the national financial network available for such purposes.

44. The credit operations of the bank must be adapted to the requirements of the export sector: (i) financing prior to shipment or consignment; (ii) short-, medium- or long-term financing subsequent to shipment or consignment. In the case of long-term transactions, account must be taken of the purchaser's credit arrangements and allowance must be made for exchange-rate fluctuations; besides, consideration must be given to the likely effect of the financing on the replacement of the international reserves of the central banks of countries which mainly encourage exports of capital goods. The bank should apply very flexible criteria with regard to interest rates, especially in the case of credits granted to sectors whose promotion is deemed desirable.

45. In addition to the proposed activities mentioned earlier, the bank would be called upon to play a very important role in the area of foodstuffs—thus acquiring certain features of a development institution. As seen by the author, through joint action of the new bank, FAO, regional development banks and other financial agencies, a vast programme of measures could be set up for developing trade and production of foodstuffs within the Third World. The foreign trade bank would be the catalyst for mobilizing these various action groups, thus ensuring the competent technical services and the necessary finance. The bank itself would provide, through national institutions, pre-finance for the export-oriented production and the credit needed for the subsequent sale and export of the foodstuffs produced.

46. The initial capital of the bank, to be subscribed by governments, is set at about US $2 billion, of which 25 per cent should be paid in cash in convertible currency and 25 per cent, again in cash, in local currency. Additional resources would come from bonds or loans floated in international capital markets, and from finance provided by subregional, regional or international banks in the following forms: (i) direct transactions through special lines of credit to stimulate exports from developing countries; (ii) complementary financing where credit is required not only for the export of products but also for capital investment in the enterprises or the projects concerned; (iii) fiduciary or administered funds provided by governmental or international organizations.

47. As can be seen, some activities of the proposed bank would go beyond the export finance area, but all the same, the creation of a new source of export finance is a major consideration underlying the proposal. As the review of the existing regional mechanisms carried out by the author tends to show, compared with other developing regions, only Latin America is in a somewhat better position, owing to the existence of such regional institutions as BLADEX. In other regions, especially in Africa, there is a conspicuous lack of regional or subregional facilities to provide effective support to national institutions.

48. A minority of countries provide credit insurance and export refinancing, though generally at short and possibly medium term. In the great majority of countries, the predominating services consist of short-term bank finance for pre-exports and exports, and these are rarely complemented by credit insurance. To finance credit to exporters, the national arrangements have to use internal resources or lines of credit from abroad. In both cases, however, the amount of finance that can be made available is affected by the requirements of other objectives of financial and monetary policies. The size of the problem assumes its true dimension when the pressing need for a drastic increase in non-traditional exports is compared with the possibility of maintaining a healthy external payments sector.

L. The bank for ACP states[19]

49. Similar considerations to those developed above have led to the proposal for the establishment of a bank for the ACP states—a project which by now has reached an advanced stage. The proposed bank will focus primarily on export financing, but it is expected that, as soon as feasible, it will also engage in activities to promote systems for export credit guarantees, insurance and reinsurance, as well as to provide appropriate technical assistance and to promote investment projects.

50. It is expected that in the early years of its operation the bank will concentrate on: (i) the creation of a market for rediscounting short-term banking acceptance generated by exports of member countries; and (ii) the offering of direct financing and refinancing for medium-term export credits.

51. Concerning the creation of an acceptance market, the bank should have the capacity to act both as an intermediary in the market and as a guarantor of the documents that it wishes to place. In the long run, however, the objective for the bank would be to act only as a complementary investor and a stimulus for expanding the secondary market. Of great importance for the development of a new acceptance market will be the bank's capacity to guarantee the payment of documents at maturity.

52. As to the medium-term operations (direct financing and refinancing), arrangements will have to be made with national organizations responsible for the medium-term financing of exports to set out the basic conditions for financing, such as the categories of exports included, the acceptable percentage of the total value, and the terms. In the case of direct financing, the institutions of exporting countries will be asked to present to the bank each individual operation, and guarantees would probably be required from official institutions of both the exporting and the importing countries.

53. The proposed technical assistance activities of the bank, envisaged for a later stage, would be concerned with: (i) the promotion of investment in projects contributing to trade development; (ii) the supply of assistance in the identification, preparation, financing, etc. of such projects; (iii) the agreements on technical assistance with other national or international institutions, etc. To provide resources for technical assistance and other promotional activities, the bank will establish a special fund for export development to be fed by voluntary contributions from the member countries and other sources.

54. The membership of the bank will be open to the governments (or designated institutions) of ACP countries, governments of the non-ACP countries, intergovernmental organizations, private commercial banks, financial organizations and companies approved by member states. The contemplated capital subscription ranges from units of account of 10 million to 20 million (three variants exist at the moment), half of which would be paid in and the other half callable.

III Payments arrangements and reserve funds

55. The idea of global mechanisms, such as a payments union and a common reserve fund, has been accepted by developing countries. However, there is a wide consensus that at this stage a direct attempt at setting up such institutions could not be very rewarding as many conditions necessary for their successful operation are still missing. As witnessed by the orientation of the work of the Co-ordination Committee of Multilateral Payments Arrangements and Monetary Co-operation among Developing Countries, it is considered that the immediate task should be to concentrate efforts on the development of appropriate forms of co-operation among the existing subregional payments and credit arrangements and on sponsoring the establishment of such facilities among new groups of countries. This largely explains why no formal proposals have been made of late for the establishment of global institutions. In the area of payments facilities, an informal proposal has been made recently by two authors for the creation of a Third World currency, as a possible instrument for stimulating the expansion of trade among developing countries.[20] The main features of the proposed scheme, which largely amounts to a payments union of a non-conventional type, will be examined in the context of proposals associated with payments arrangements. Following this, the situation in the area of credit arrangements will be examined, with particular reference to the proposals submitted to the Co-ordination Committee. Some special facilities recently established in two subregions will be also reviewed in this context.

M. Payments arrangements

(a) *A global payments union*

56. The last proposal for a global payments union, which, however, has not given rise to any further action, dates back to 1976. The proposal constitutes the major part of a study prepared as a contribution for the Action Programme for Economic Co-operation among Non-Aligned Countries.[21] The proposed scheme, with its revolving credit mechanism composed of contributions in convertible currencies, is basically a replica of the former European Payments Union, with most technical issues left open for negotiation among governments.

The payments union proper was complemented by a common reserve fund supposed to act as 'the second line of defence'. A more detailed review of the proposal would add little to what is already known of the general features of conventional payments unions.

57. The feasibility of a payments union among developing countries continues to be discussed mainly in academic circles, although it may be remarked that studies in depth are conspicuously lacking. More recently, the subject has been discussed at some length in a study produced by the Centre for Research on the New International Economic Order, which has tried to elaborate a framework for the financial and monetary co-operation of developing countries. The authors consider a global payments union as an essential element of such co-operation, but they abstain from formulating a more precise proposal.[22]

58. The problems and difficulties which would be likely to impede the smooth functioning of a global payments union have been reviewed in several reports submitted to the Co-ordination Committee; notably, the lack of complementarity between developing countries associated with undiversified production structures, inelasticity of supply, lack of established economic ties outside relatively small groups of neighbouring countries with similar history and tradition, etc.; but almost invariably the emphasis is laid on the problem of persistent surpluses which, according to all reports, would inevitably emerge. As put in a report, 'the idea of a global payments union of the conventional type would not appear to be feasible, given the perfectly justified reluctance of most developing countries to expose themselves to the danger of accumulating inconvertible balances in their international reserves.'[23] The report concludes by stating that 'the outlook for stronger and wider monetary co-operation among developing countries must be based on those types of multilateral arrangements which, without initially producing spectacular results, have been or are being tested in actual practice and do not entail unrealistic financial or political commitments.'

59. The Co-ordination Committee has discussed the feasibility

of a global payments union. It has recognized the merits of a global scheme but has arrived at the conclusion that it should be 'regarded as too ambitious for the time being.'[24]

60. The present work of the Committee, characterized by a gradual and pragmatic approach, is largely concentrated on the identification and establishment of possible links between the existing subregional clearing arrangements which, taken together, cover close to fifty countries.[25] The basic principles governing this work are: (i) the independence and autonomy of each arrangement has to be fully respected; and (ii) no link can be established if it is not supported by existing or potential trade flows. Initially it had been proposed to establish direct links between arrangements, though—at least in the beginning—on a bilateral rather than on a multilateral basis. However, in view of the pronounced specific features of individual clearing arrangements, an indirect route had to be adopted, namely, to link individual countries with individual clearing arrangements, thus enabling a country to participate in two or more arrangements. A set of rules for this procedure has been worked out and submitted for consideration to the clearing arrangements. The most important of these rules concerns interim finance. The latter is to 'be based on credit lines agreed upon bilaterally between pairs of participants in different regional arrangements without precluding the possibility of global credit lines granted by a single country to all or to groups of countries participating in other regional systems.'[26]

N. A common currency of developing countries

61. The proposal for a more flexible trade-promoting mechanism for the Third World, mentioned earlier, was formulated in an article published in the 1980 Autumn issue of the UNCTAD Trade and Development Review.[27] The main features of the proposed scheme can be summarized as follows:

(i) An institution to be set up by developing countries and run by a Board of Management, should issue new currency units (NCUs) for the payment of an agreed portion of the mutually traded goods and services. The scheme would run for a period of possibly three years, with provision for a review after the first two years of operation. Like the

SDRs, the NCUs should consist of book entries in ledgers, kept by the secretariat, under the supervision of the Board.

(ii) The allocation of the NCUs among the participating countries should be based on agreed criteria such as, for instance, the IMF quotas. The proportion of the total export receipts would have to be worked out, but for the sake of illustration, the authors assume a 25 per cent formula—the rest to be paid as before in convertible currencies.

(iii) Whether the scheme would cover all exports or only specified categories (such as manufactures) would be a matter of agreement. As a possible solution, the authors suggest the exemption of one or two specified commodities. The authors point out, however, that countries which have plentiful hard currency markets for their exports would not gain much from the scheme, and would be unlikely to join except as part of a strategy to support Third World co-operation.

(iv) Countries which run down their NCU balances below the initial level would pay interest, while countries which accumulate balances would receive interest. However, the interest rate ought not to be too high as the purpose of the scheme is to encourage countries to spend their NCUs, and not to hold idle balances.

62. Prima facie, some features of the proposed scheme look rather attractive. Every participating country would be a potential gainer, in that it would acquire purchasing power over the goods of other developing countries. On the other hand, there would be no compulsion on any country to sell goods to other participants if hard currency markets were available. What is particularly important, the scheme could operate irrespective of the system of trade or foreign exchange control of the participating countries. Countries would be free to impose restrictions whenever economic conditions so required. Furthermore, the problems posed by the existence of subregional payments schemes would be much easier to deal with than in the case of a conventional payments union. Countries which are members of such schemes could hold NCUs individually; or—especially in the case of more advanced schemes—the new currency could be held and used by the

subregional schemes themselves. All this should make the negotiation of an agreement considerably easier than the negotiation of a conventional payments union. Besides, the proposed scheme would be relatively easy to operate.

63. Difficulties arise, however, when it comes to the problem of surpluses. As under any global payments schemes, some countries would be likely to develop persistent surpluses—with large amounts of accumulated NCUs—others persistent deficits.

64. The authors begin by stating that a highly unbalanced situation would be likely to generate some self-correcting effects. The surplus countries would have an incentive to buy more from other participants, and the deficit countries would have an incentive to divert part of their exports to other members of the scheme. Aware that self-adjustment would not proceed far by itself, the authors consider a number of measures, including hard currency backing, but they dismiss them one after another. They end up by suggesting a progressive scaling down of the proportion of NCUs in the total export receipts which countries with increasing NCUs balances would be required to accept—for example, 20 per cent at a given level, 15 per cent at a higher level, and so on until an agreed ceiling was reached.

65. The authors in fact fail to produce a satisfactory answer to the problem of accumulated NCU balances, which they themselves consider as crucial. The suggested scaling-down procedure could slow down the process and might act as a timely warning to the countries concerned, but by itself it would not prevent the surpluses reaching an agreed ceiling, thus leaving the problem open as before. To the extent that a solution could be found at all, more active measures would have to be considered such as, for instance, imposing time limits on extreme creditor and debtor positions, increasing the interest rate for countries which ran down their NCU balances over long periods and—if at all workable—introducing interest payments on accumulating balances exceeding an agreed period. The question, however, is whether any of these measures could produce the desired effects without introducing at some point the use of convertible currencies—an expedient which the authors would like to avoid as it might lessen the attractiveness of the scheme.

O. Reserve funds

(b) *A Third World reserve fund*

66. The situation concerning proposals in this particular area is not very difficult from that in the area of payments arrangements. The need for a Third World source of balance of payments finance has been recognized, but an attempt at this stage to build up a single common institution is not considered very realistic. Clearly, the establishment of a common reserve fund would not be associated with the same technical difficulties as a global payments union; but to provide effective help to countries the institution would have to be endowed with sufficiently large resources in convertible currencies. Taken as a group, developing countries could mobilize the resources needed, but only on the condition that the few financially strong countries were prepared to assume the bulk of the burden.

67. A case for a Third World reserve fund was made in the 1976 study on a global payments union mentioned earlier.[28] The author of the study has had in mind a large-scale institution operated by developing countries. However, in addition to the contributions of the participating countries and special contributions from OPEC sources, the study was counting on additional concessional finance from developing countries which, at the time of writing, may have looked a reasonable assumption. The study had implicitly assumed that the use of resources and conditionality under the proposed scheme would be virtually the same as those practised by the IMF.

68. The already quoted study of the NIEO Research Centre[29] is very much in favour of a global reserve fund entirely financed by developing countries. Such an institution would not only make a contribution to the much needed balance of payments finance, but would also provide developing countries with an opportunity to put into effect 'alternative conditionality'. As the authors of the study see it, 'the first principle of conditionality', which is the repayment in the medium term, must be ensured. But instead of using uniform policy prescriptions to enforce this principle, a Third World institution would have to devise alternative policy packages applicable to different political, social and economic conditions. According to the

study, special contributions by the OPEC members would be essential for setting up a viable reserve fund.

69. Suggestions along similar lines can be found in a number of articles coming from academic sources, but hardly any of them sheds new light on the problem. In a recent article,[30] for instance, opinion is expressed that developing countries have the financial capacity to set up their own monetary fund provided that the OPEC member countries are prepared to take the leading role. Acting together, the Third World should be able to mobilize some US $10 billion which, according to the author, would be sufficient to run operations for a period of about four years. A part of the subscriptions—and the same goes for borrowings—should be made in domestic currencies, which would act as a stimulus to trade among developing countries. The author also argues for new conditionality rules and procedures adapted to the complex realities of the Third World.

P. The actual proposals

70. Proposals from official quarters put the accent on the promotion of appropriate co-operation forms among the existing subregional credit arrangements,[31] pointing out that the approach should be both selective and gradual. As put in a report submitted to the Co-ordination Committee, 'although from the technical point of view the existing credit arrangements among developing countries show a higher degree of uniformity than the clearing arrangements, the possibility of introducing meaningful links or combinations is less certain.'[32] Two arguments are advanced in support of this statement: first, regional credit arrangements have been largely fashioned according to specific balance of payments needs, and these differ considerably from country to country; and secondly, the surveillance of economic policies associated with conditionality, which is an outstanding feature of these arrangements and has political implications, cannot be easily shared with non-member countries.

71. The proposals submitted to the Co-ordination Committee are generally in agreement that among the various possible steps priority should be given to:

(i) the promotion of reciprocal investments among subregional reserve funds (which in the beginning would be easiest to achieve among the Arab Monetary Fund, the Central American Stabilization Fund and the Andean Reserve Fund);

(ii) the establishment of regular contacts among arrangements at technical levels, in view of improving and harmonizing lending policies, and more particularly, the principles of conditionality applied by the different credit arrangements;

(iii) organized support through technical expertise and co-operation to the setting up of new credit mechanisms in other developing regions and areas.

It should also be mentioned that suggestions have been made to study the possibility within the prevailing features of each region of linking the use of a percentage of the arrangements' revenues in the finance of member countries' exports.[33]

72. A proposal which deserves attention, although it has not been worked out in detail, concerns the establishment of what its sponsor calls '*a financial security network*' among developing countries.[34] The immediate objective of this 'network' would be to provide additional balance of payments finance, not through the creation of a global institution, but through a close co-operation of the central banks of the countries concerned, with the assistance of regional financial institutions. Pledges by governments or central banks should make available the agreed amount of resources. These resources could be used either by means of direct drawing upon them, or through the issue of securities in financial markets guaranteed by the country drawn against.

Q. The orientation of the Committee's work

73. The Co-ordination Committee which, as a first step, had examined in detail the objectives, institutional features and policies of the existing credit arrangements, is presently engaged in: (i) the formulation of terms and principles which would enable the subregional institutions to establish mutual financial support schemes; and (ii) the exploration of conditionality principles best suited to developing countries, which could be adopted by all subregional arrangements.

74. Regarding the establishment of mutual support schemes, two modalities[35] are presently considered as promising: (i) direct bilateral deposits between credit arrangements, and (ii) indirect support through investment with international banking institutions, which would in turn provide financial support to subregional credit institutions in need of funds (noting, however, that the viability of this procedure should be assessed in the light of requirements of market conditions and the possibility of avoiding collateral commitments and concessions). The terms and conditions which would be likely to enhance the interest of the potential lending institutions in the mutual support schemes have been defined by the Committee as follows: (i) the potential borrowers should enjoy an independent legal status, to be able to enter as principals a valid loan contract; (ii) the central banks of the members of a borrowing credit arrangement should be prepared to provide adequate guarantees for the funds supplied by other credit institutions; (iii) the potential borrowers should be in a position to issue negotiable market instruments of such maturities which are suitable to the potential lenders; and (iv) interest rates applicable to loans obtained under the mutual support schemes should be in line with rates in the Euromarket.[36] The application of these terms and conditions, however, will require adjustments in the status and operations of certain credit arrangements and, occasionally, in the operations of national institutions as well.[37]

75. Regarding the problems associated with conditionality, all proposals recently submitted to the Committee are in agreement that the principle of conditionality should continue to be applied by the subregional credit institution, but they have strong reservations on the present approach to balance of payments adjustment policies, with its emphasis on demand management. What most proposals ask for is a co-ordination between development financing and balance of payments support facilities, implying that the use of the latter should be based on development plans acceptable both to the borrowing countries and to the lending institutions. In other words, 'the criteria for balance of payments support should be related to an assessment of the viability of medium-term development plans and the monitoring of their implementation.'[38] As agreed by the

Committee at its last meeting, an appropriate theoretical and operational framework for this co-ordinated approach to the balance of payments and development finance will have to be elaborated by the joint efforts of the Technical Secretariat and the subregional credit arrangements, with the help of appropriate international organizations.

R. Some special credit facilities

76. Although actually in operation, some specially conceived subregional credit facilities should be recalled in the present context, as they might serve as examples of co-operation to be followed by other groups of developing countries.

77. The facility created by the agreement which had been signed in August 1980 by the Presidents of Mexico and Venezuela deserves particular attention. Under the terms of this agreement, known as the Energy Co-operation Programme for Central American and Caribbean Countries, the two oil-exporting countries supply a combined 160,000 barrels of oil per day on concessionary terms to Barbados, Costa Rica, El Salvador, Guatemala, Honduras, Jamaica, Nicaragua, Panama and the Dominican Republic. The oil supply covers up to one half of the needs of the countries listed, later joined by Belize, and 30 per cent of its total value consists of credits granted by Mexico and Venezuela for a period of five years, charged at an interest rate of only 4 per cent. At the beginning of August 1981, the governments of the two oil-exporting countries decided to extend the agreement for one more year. It is also reported that Mexico and Venezuela are presently exploring the feasibility of constructing a joint oil refinery, in Central America or the Caribbean, which would cover the future energy needs of the whole region.

78. Reference should also be made to the joint action by Trinidad and Tobago to establish a facility for the purchase of oil, fertilizers and asphalt by countries of the Caribbean subregion. The idea is to use the incremental cost of these purchases (taking 1 January 1979 as the index base) to be rolled back, in the form of programme loans, to the purchasing countries. It is expected that over two years the facility could provide Trinidad and Tobago with an amount of about US $220 million.

Notes

1. Dr Mohamed W. Khouja, 'Towards a Strategy for Economic Co-operation between the Arab Oil-Producing Countries and the Third World', mimeograph, 1979.
2. This refers in particular to the 1978 Mexican proposal for the establishment of a $15 billion fund which was supposed to be disbursed in the form of long-term loans. The loans could only be used to purchase capital goods from those developed countries whose governments had contributed to the bond issue supposed to finance the fund.
3. The proposal was submitted for the first time to UNCTAD V, Manila, May 1979.
4. There is no indication in the proposal whether, in the calculation of the contributions to be made by the donor countries, the incidence of the changes of the export prices of non-oil developing countries would also be taken into account.
5. Joint proposal submitted by the Algerian and Venezuelan delegations to the meeting of OPEC Ministers held in Caracas in December 1979.
6. Actually, at the time of submission of the proposal, these assets were of the order of $1 billion, but in its introductory part the proposal has made a case for increasing them up to $4 billion in 1980.
7. The role of joint ventures between Arab oil-exporting countries and other developing countries is strongly emphasized in the already-quoted study by Dr Mohamed W. Khouja and in some other studies from Arab sources, like those summarized in proposal D.
8. *A New Vision of Financial Relations*, Zuhayr Mikdashi, Professor at the School of Business Administration of the University of Lausanne, and Secretary-General of the Arab-European Business Council, European Management Forum, Geneva, Switzerland, 1981.
9. An important exception, however, refers to energy exploration. Loans made for this particular purpose should not be reimbursed if they did not give rise to commercially viable projects.
10. Zuhair Mikdashi, 'Oil Prices and OPEC Surpluses: Some Reflections', *International Affairs*, 1980.
11. Kamal Hossain, *Financial Flows from the Arab Middle East to sub-Saharan Africa: Assessment and Prospects*. Centre for Research on the New International Economic Order, Oxford, 1980.
12. R. L. Martinez, 'Monetary and Financial Co-operation to support the Programme of Trade Preferences among Developing Countries' (TD/B/C.7/27, 22 March 1979).
13. Leelananda de Silva, 'A commercial and merchant bank of developing countries' (abridged version). International Workshop on the Promotion of Economic and Technical Co-operation among Developing Countries, Bled, Yugoslavia, November 1981. (The full version in a draft form is available in mimeographed form.)

14. Report on an Expert Group Meeting on New and Renewable Sources of Energy, Castel Gandolfo, Rome, May 1981.
15. Detailed Operation of an Export Credit Guarantee Facility (TD/B/AC.33/L.2, 21 January 1982).
16. Framework for International Financial Co-operation, Centre for Research on the New International Economic Order, Oxford, 1981. Also, A. Sengupta, 'The Structure of International Finance and the Less Developed Economics' (unpublished paper, written in 1977).
17. Rodrigo Florente Martinez, *Monetary and Financial Co-operation to support the Programme of Trade Preferences among Developing Countries* (TD/B/C.7/27, March 1979).
18. Ibid.
19. *Intra-ACP Co-operation*, Supplementary Study on the Project for establishing a Bank for ACP States, Brussels, 9 June 1981.
20. An earlier version of this proposal was discussed by an UNCTAD Group of Experts in October/November 1975. The Group of Experts recommended that 'the proposal to create a special monetary unit issued to, and acceptable by, developing countries should be further explored. . . . Such a proposal would be in line with the spirit of collective self-reliance and might avoid some of the difficulties encountered by more complex arrangements.' (TD/B/AC.19/1, para. 37.)
21. A. R. Abdel Meguid, 'A Proposal for the Finance and Expansion of Trade among Developing Countries (A Global Payments Union)', July 1976.
22. Centre for Research on NIEO, 'Framework for International Financial Co-operation', Oxford, June 1981.
23. Jorge Gonzales del Valle, Preliminary Report on the Feasibility of Global Payments Arrangements among Developing Countries (TD/B/C.7/26, 1978).
24. Report of the third meeting of the Co-ordination Committee, p. 6.
25. The existing clearing arrangements comprise: (i) the West African Clearing Union (13 members); (ii) the Caricom Multilateral Clearing Facility (6 members); (iii) the Central American Clearing House (5 members); (iv) the Regional Co-operation for Development Union for Multilateral Payments Arrangements (3 members); (v) the LAFTA Payments System (12 members); (vi) the Asian Clearing Union (7 members); (vii) the Central African Clearing House (3 members). In addition, nine countries of eastern and southern Africa signed a treaty in December 1981 establishing a preferential trade area complemented with a clearing arrangement and a common Trade and Development Bank. This treaty, which may be joined by a few more countries, is the outcome of the Declaration of Intent and Commitment to the establishment of a Preferential Trade Area for Eastern and Southern African States, signed in March 1978 in Lusaka by seventeen countries.

26. Report of the fourth meeting of the Co-ordination Committee, p. 16.
27. Frances Stuart and Michael Stuart, 'A new currency for trade among developing Countries', UNCTAD *Trade and Development Review*, No. 2, August 1980.
28. A. R. Abdel Meguid, op. cit.
29. Centre for Research on the New International Economic Order, op. cit.
30. Richard L. Kitchen, 'Alternative possibilities for handling balance of payments and debt crises', in International Foundation for Development Alternatives Dossier No. 25, September/October 1981.
31. The existing credit arrangements comprise: (i) the Arab Monetary Fund (20 members); (ii) the Andean Reserve Fund (5 members); (iii) the Central American Monetary Stabilization Fund (5 members); (iv) the Latin American Free Trade Association's Financial Assistance Agreement (12 members); (v) the ASEAN Group Arrangement (5 members). The West African Monetary Union has a pool of monetary reserves to which each member country has access. The CARICOM Multilateral Clearing Facility has recently set up its own credit mechanism.
32. J. G. del Valle, op. cit. (TD/B/C.7/26, 1978).
33. Report of the Working Group on Credit Arrangements among Developing Countries, pp. 9–10, Bogota, Colombia, July 1980.
34. R. L. Martinez, op. cit. (TD/B/C.7/27, March 1979).
35. The establishment of mutual swap arrangements was considered as a third possibility. It appeared, however, that such arrangements would not be particularly helpful 'as they essentially involve exchange of obligations denominated in local currencies of the participants concerned which are not dealt with by credit arrangements.' Report of the fourth meeting of the Co-ordination Committee, p. 18.
36. Report of the fourth meeting of the Co-ordination Committee, p. 19.
37. Some of the existing credit arrangements do not possess an independent legal status; the constitutions of most central banks usually contain restrictions on their ability to provide guarantee on loans involving third parties; and there are many restrictions on the ability of certain credit institutions to issue negotiable securities of short maturity. Ibid.
38. Ibid., p. 26.

4 JOINT VENTURES AMONG DEVELOPING COUNTRIES

J. D. A. CUDDY

Introduction

1. There is growing recognition in the oil-exporting countries that the geographical distribution of both of their foreign investments and of their imports, especially of manufactured goods, has been too heavily concentrated in recent years in the industrial countries. From the perspective of these countries, a diversification both of the destinations of foreign investments and of the sources of imports could lead to considerable economic gains. Concurrently, such a diversification, if directed towards other developing countries, could under the appropriate conditions greatly stimulate the economic growth of these latter countries, with a resulting multiplier effect on world growth generally. There are, however, good reasons for the existing concentration of investments and import sourcing, among which the relative stability of purchasing power in the industrial countries on the one hand, and the lack of appropriate vehicles for investment and the development of export sources in the developing countries on the other hand, bulk large. Whilst it can be argued that the attractiveness of investments and import sourcing in the industrial countries has declined significantly in recent years, as a result both of the threat of asset-freezing and the rapid escalation of export prices (at least to the oil-exporting countries), the purpose of this note is not to argue this case, but to discuss the second point regarding investment and import sourcing in developing countries. This is a specific aspect of the more general issue of economic co-operation among developing countries. A note on resource complementarity between OPEC and non-OPEC developing countries is attached (Annexe 4.1).

2. Many developing countries which are now primarily dependent

upon commodity exports lack the capital, technical, managerial and marketing skills for undertaking manufacturing or value-added activities for export, and would welcome, subject to their policies on foreign collaboration, opportunities for export development. Others, including the oil-exporting countries, possess sufficient capital but are concerned to rely too heavily on a limited range of suppliers, particularly for technologically complex imports. Such concerns stimulate the search for mechanisms to enhance economic co-operation among these countries. However, such proposals—encompassing, among others, customs unions, common markets, regional planning and development institutions—have not been notably successful.

The joint venture

3. By contrast with the traditional approaches, it would appear that an alternative vehicle, the joint venture (JV) on a commercial basis, involving a partnership between public and private investors, multinational corporations (MNCs) and 'host' government(s), holds significant attraction. The reasons for this conclusion may be briefly summarized.

(a) JVs are 'active' (rather than merely 'permissive' as in the case of traditional schemes). Commercial viability and therefore the jobs of management depend upon their ability to formulate, evaluate and implement 'bankable' projects, a lack of capacity for which is usually cited as a severe bottleneck in developing countries;
(b) JVs can be very flexible in size, ownership structure and capital structure, both initially and over time;
(c) JVs also, by making direct and concrete investment and production decisions, actively create employment and trade opportunities;
(d) since they necessarily involve commercial partners in different countries, JVs are particularly suited to exploiting dynamic resource complementarities, leading to more efficient resource allocation both instantaneously and over time;
(e) JVs can serve as active innovating agents by direct transfer of suitable technology, management and marketing skills, thus indigenizing self-supporting growth potential;

(f) since JVs enjoy a comparative advantage in identifying profitable additional investment opportunities, their savings and investment ratios are likely to be higher than those of alternative enterprises, thus ultimately increasing national savings (and hence growth) rates in the economies in which they operate. This in turn would lead to a more diversified and higher yielding asset portfolio for investors in the JVs.

4. The basis for JVs is the commercial exploitation of dynamic resource complementarities. Accordingly, projects undertaken by them would be likely to concentrate initially on sectors in which the developing countries enjoy comparative factor cost advantages (primarily the production and processing of agricultural products and industrial raw materials and the labour-intensive and standardized-technology sectors, such as food, textiles and garments, machine tools, electromechanical products, the paper and rubber industries, footwear, and cosmetics). However, many developing countries have already reached high standards in the production of technology-intensive goods (such as telephone equipment, diesel engines, measuring instruments, automotive equipment and durable consumer goods) and JVs in such areas would seem particularly well suited to the needs of many oil-exporting developing countries.

Constraints on the development of JVs

5. Given the advantages and potential cited above of commercially-based JVs among developing countries, the question arises why they have not yet developed on a broad basis. Several factors appear to be at the root of this, including:

(a) lack of information about investment opportunities and resource and market complementarities;
(b) shortage of entrepreneurial experience in presenting projects as being bankable;
(c) perception by potential investors of substantial non-commercial risks in investment in developing countries;
(d) lack of an institutional framework for the generation of financing for bankable JVs; and
(e) legal barriers resulting from lack of harmonization of

national laws relating to taxation, control, incentives, repatriation of profits, and reinvestments.

Proposed institutional framework

6. Many of the constraints cited above could be overcome by the establishment of an appropriate institutional framework for the promotion of joint ventures among developing countries. Such a framework would need to include:

(a) a clearing-house for information on existing JVs and on markets, resources and legal structures in member countries;
(b) the provision of pre-project technical assistance (financial structuring, technical engineering studies, identification of prospective markets and suppliers, determination of key staffing requirements) and of appraisal for fully-developed project proposals;
(c) a mechanism for the supply of investment guarantees and export credit finance to enhance the attractiveness of JVs in sectors and countries with which potential investors may be unfamiliar;
(d) a mechanism for bringing together potential investors (public and private investors from member countries, host governments, and MNCs) and other sources of funds (e.g. commercial banks);
(e) a capital base for the provision of direct equity and/or loan finance to approved JVs.

Each of these functions is being carried out to some extent already by existing institutions, but what is lacking is a co-ordinated approach to all five functions jointly, and an emphasis on directing these functions towards the promotion of joint ventures. This implies the need for a single focal point of such activities, which might be viewed as something like a 'South-South IFC'.[1] It could involve itself either as a direct investor in an approved JV, or as a broker, bringing together various sources of finance whilst not engaging its own funds directly. By constrast with the IFC, however, the proposed institution would view its investments in JVs as long term in nature.

7. The proposed institution would enable potential investors to

diversify their investment portfolios in commercially-sound ventures across a broad range of developing countries. It would concomitantly reduce the concentration in a few hands of investments in individual countries, which should encourage such countries to liberalize their foreign investment climates. Potential investors could participate directly in approved JVs, as suppliers of equity or loans in the financing of specific projects sponsored by the institution, or indirectly as participants in the capital base of the institution, which would itself be investing in some of the sponsored projects.

Capital structure

8. Participation in the capital base of the proposed institution should be attractive to potential investors in view of the avowedly commercial focus of the joint ventures which such an institution would promote. Moreover, the necessary capital base need not entail significant amounts of paid-in capital since the preponderant part of the institution's use of funds would consist in investments in bankable joint ventures, for which funds should be readily available from capital markets. Thus, a capital structure involving, say, a conservative 1:10 ratio between paid-in and callable capital should be more than adequate to support the institution's operations. Moreover, earnings made by the institution on its investments could, in some measure, be returned to its shareholders in the form of dividend payments.

9. An attractive alternative to the capital structure just discussed could be the inclusion of the proposed JV institution within a broader merchant bank whose primary functions would be essentially similar, but which would not be confined to joint ventures. Such a bank would have the advantage of participating directly in international capital markets and could attempt to expand and locate new sources of capital both for JVs and for other projects, particularly in countries which have had very little banking contacts with the developing countries (e.g., the Nordic countries, and the several thousand US banks which have no international arms at present). It could also profitably develop sound commercial intelligence and financial advice capacities which could both reduce reliance on multinational

banks based in the industrial countries, and strengthen the financial management capacities of the corporate sector in developing countries.

10. If managed on strict commercial lines, such a bank should be profitable, as the earnings reports of similar existing banks readily attest. Its capital structure could initially be along the lines suggested above for the proposed JV institution. Since, however, the ratio of capital plus reserves to total assets of several major established banks with extensive interests in the developing countries is even lower (5–8 per cent or less, implying at least a 1:12 ratio between paid-in and callable capital) the merchant bank, once properly established, might be able to expand significantly the scale of its operations without the need for further capital injections.

Possible finance requirements

11. Analysis by the World Bank and other financial institutions indicates that over the period 1980–5, the gap between domestically-generated savings, and total investment requirements in oil-importing developing countries is likely to be in the range of 3–4 per cent of GDP. These same institutions anticipate that, account having been taken of workers' remittances, interest payments and other current transactions, approximately one-half of these net foreign capital requirements would be met by ODA, multilateral sources, official export credits, changes in reserves and short-term borrowings. The remainder would have to come from private medium- and long-term borrowing, and private direct investment. A large and growing proportion of private borrowings is devoted to amortization and interest repayments; little is left to finance new investments and probably only a very small part of even this residual would be in the form of borrowings abroad by established joint ventures. This leaves private direct investment as the major source of foreign finance for joint ventures. Although it is extremely difficult to obtain information on the scale of joint venture finance historically, the recent experience of such institutions as the IFC suggests that joint ventures would constitute not more than 5–10 per cent of this total.

12. Supposing that the proposed new institution were ambitiously to seek to double the amount of available joint venture finance, this would imply a required capitalization on the order of 10 per cent of the total of private direct investment in the oil-importing developing countries over the period of interest, which is taken here to be the three years 1983–5. Based upon World Bank projections for the World Development Report (1981), this latter total for 1983–5 would be in the region of $60 billion, of which 10 per cent would be $6 billion. However, these projections are based upon balance of payments data whose use to estimate the requirements for joint venture finance could be misleading, for two main reasons. First, such data are on a net basis, whereas gross flows are more relevant here. Second, for tax reasons much investment by TNCs is shifted by internal accounting procedures from the direct investment to the private borrowing category. Such spotty evidence as is available suggests that the estimates should be at least doubled to take these factors into account. On this basis, the total capitalization of the proposed new institution would be $12 billion and if the 1:10 ratio of paid-in to callable capital suggested in the text were applied, the paid-in capital would be $1.1 billion and the callable $10.9 billion, making a total of $12 billion.

13. As it will take time for the new institution to develop its operations, even assuming an aggressive initiative (which we are assuming), a phasing of the above paid-in amount over several years is indicated.

Annexe 4.1

Resource complementarity between OPEC and NOPEC[2]

1. During the decade of the 1970s, OPEC as a trade market expanded dramatically, total imports increasing from about $9.5 billion in 1970 to nearly $99 billion in 1979, an *annual* rate of growth of approximately 30 per cent. The distribution of these imports as between food and manufactures, the two major categories, remained roughly stable over the period, food accounting for about 12.5 per cent of the total in 1979, and manufactures about 71 per cent. What is more interesting from

the viewpoint of resource complementarity, however, is the distribution within product groups across suppliers. Thus, although DMECs maintain their shares of food and manufactures imports over the period (accounting for about 65 per cent of food and 84 per cent of manufactures imports), the NOPEC countries were able to increase their share for the same product categories; their share of food imports rose from 9.4 to 12.8 per cent, and of manufactures from 6.5 to 9.5 per cent. These gains were achieved almost entirely at the expense of the socialist countries of Eastern Europe (although the dynamism of OPEC imports was such that even these latter countries' exports of food and manufactures to OPEC grew in value at annual rates of 21 per cent each).

2. It is thus clear that the NOPEC countries are becoming increasingly competitive in the OPEC markets, although the OPEC countries continue to rely heavily on the exports of the DMEC countries. Whilst this is perhaps understandable for OPEC imports of manufactures, it is less clear why the DMEC countries should so dominate in food imports. Moreover, as Table 1 shows, this dominance persists even for the categories of agricultural raw materials, and ores and metals, products which the NOPEC countries would seem to be in a position to supply competitively.

3. Examination of the trade statistics published by the OECD at the 3-digit SITC level[3] indicates that within the three categories just mentioned, the major products exported by DMECs to the OPEC countries are: dairy products (milk, cream, butter, cheese); cereals (wheat and wheat flour, rice, cereal preparations); beverages (both alcoholic and non-alcoholic); tobacco; fixed vegetable oils (soft); railway sleepers; textile fibres; fertilizers, iron and steel (ingots, rods, bars, plates, sheets, tubes and pipes); copper; and aluminium. Trade statistics published by UNCTAD, also at the 3-digit SITC level,[4] indicate that, with the exception of railway sleepers, all of these products are also exported by developing countries. This suggests a very considerable resource complementarity between OPEC and NOPEC countries in these non-manufacturing sectors, where the degree of product differentiation is not nearly so great as for manufactured products. Moreover, since OPEC imports in these three

Table 1 Structure of OPEC imports (percentage shares of total)

Product group		Origin		
		DMEC	NOPEC	Socialist Europe
1. Food	1970	65.3	24.7	7.2
	1979	64.5	26.3	4.0
2. Agricultural raw materials	1970	75.6	12.8	7.7
	1979	58.7	28.1	9.9
3. Ores and metals	1970	80.7	11.5	7.0
	1979	80.5	15.7	3.0
4 Manufactures	1970	84.8	6.4	6.9
	1979	84.1	9.5	3.8

Source: UNCTAD secretariat calculations.

Table 2 Structure of OPEC imports from NOPEC (percentage shares of total)

Product Group		Origin		
		Africa	South-East Asia	Latin America
1. Food	1970	6.7	10.9	3.2
	1979	3.9	13.3	6.9
2. Agricultural raw materials	1970	2.6	7.7	3.0
	1979	3.5	14.3	9.7
3. Ores and metals	1970	0.9	6.7	2.6
	1979	0.2	8.1	4.0
4. Manufactures	1970	0.7	3.8	0.8
	1979	0.3	6.4	1.7

Source: UNCTAD secretariat calculations.

sectors (food, agricultural raw materials, and ores and metals) have been rising at well over 25 per cent per annum and amounted to approximately $22 billion in 1979, of which about $15 billion was supplied by DMEC countries, it is clear that both OPEC and NOPEC countries could benefit substantially from a concerted attempt to shift the geographical distribution of import sourcing for these sectors in the future.

4. As to the manufacturing sector, where import growth has been even faster (30 per cent per annum), reaching over $70 billion in 1979, the statistical sources quoted above indicate that substantial complementarity appears to exist in a number of manufacturing sectors as well. This is particularly true for chemicals, machinery, electronic equipment, road vehicles and other transport equipment, in addition to the traditional areas of textiles, clothing, footwear and household appliances. Although the DMECs hold the distinct advantage in these sectors (as in other manufactured goods) of established reputations associated with sophisticated marketing techniques and product identification via the use of 'brand names', the very fact that many DMEC firms operating in these sectors have either established production facilities in the developing countries or clamoured for protection from competitive goods produced in the developing countries argues strongly for the existence of a substantial cost advantage to import sourcing in these latter countries.

5. The conclusions reached above concerning existing resource complementarity need to be qualified because of the relatively high level of aggregation of the trade statistics examined, which necessarily gloss over the detail of product differentiation. However, it is doubtful that further study of trade data would serve much purpose since the product categories employed even in the most detailed trade statistics available are still too crude for practical commercial purposes. It would seem to be far more efficient to entrust the exploitation of such resource complementarity as appears to exist to project promoters, developers and entrepreneurs, encouraging them by the provision of both technical assistance in project preparation and, where necessary, export credits and loan or equity finance.

6. Finally, it should be noted that the expansion of trade links

among developing countries would in itself encourage the creation of *dynamic* resource complementarity, particularly as facilities for mineral and energy exploration and exploitation were developed, and technological sophistication in manufacturing sectors were both diffused among partners and expanded, perhaps partly through interchanges with partners from the industrial countries.

Notes

1. The guarantee and the export credit functions are sufficiently differentiated from the rest, however, to call perhaps for separate institutional co-arrangements, but still within the same essentially South-South family.
2. The term NOPEC is used as a shorthand for the oil-importing developing countries. In the text, the term DMEC is used to refer to the Western industrialized countries.
3. OECD, *Trade by Commodities January–December 1979*, Paris, 1981.
4. UNCTAD, *Handbook of International Trade and Development Statistics, Supplement 1980*, New York, 1980, table 4.3(C).

5 EXPORT CREDIT

J. D. A. CUDDY

Introduction

1. Recent years have witnessed an increasing emphasis by developing countries on the expansion of exports as a dynamic factor in overall growth providing both domestic employment and needed foreign exchange. Given the well-known income inelasticity of exports of primary products, this emphasis has necessarily entailed a diversification of exports away from such 'traditional' areas into manufactured goods. Although considerable success has been achieved by a dozen developing countries in a range of such manufactures exports, most developing countries have experienced considerable difficulties in achieving the needed diversification. There are many reasons for this, but one is that the financing of such exports presents a problem. By contrast with traditional commodity exports to traditional markets, which are either self-financing or attractive to foreign financing since traded on international exchanges with quoted prices, standardized grades and well-established procedures, non-traditional exports require types of financing which are much less readily available through conventional sources, domestic or international.

2. Such exports face competition in many sectors from developed countries which subsidize exports via national export finance institutions or which have access to ample sources of finance in international markets at interest rates which reflect the lower country-risk premiums associated with these countries. Moreover, since export credits amount in fact to loans to foreign buyers, they represent an export of capital which most developing countries can ill afford, and which is not reversed until the importer liquidates the loan. It therefore seems imperative that attention is devoted to possible means to mitigate these problems faced by developing countries as they

attempt to expand their exports. Finally, even when developing countries expand the exports of their traditional products to new markets, e.g. to other developing countries, they may face export financing difficulties as the buyers are not known to the banks normally financing such exports. Thus it is the exports of new products to both old and new markets, and of old products to new markets, which face shortages of finance, although in differing degrees.

Existing mechanisms

3. The major sources of export credits in developing countries are the commercial banks. Whilst, as indicated, these banks are readily prepared to finance 'traditional' exports to traditional markets, for non-traditional exports—mainly manufactures—the size and maturities of individual transactions, the creditworthiness of the borrowers, the rates of interest which they can pay, and the type of goods which require financing are not within the range which existing banks have in the past been readily willing to accept. In particular, whereas the maturity of export credits for traditional exports rarely exceeds 180 days, the reverse is true for non-traditional exports, many of which require credit for medium-term periods (between one and five years) and sometimes (especially for major capital goods and 'turnkey' projects) up to ten or twelve years. The longer the terms required, the greater the burden on the developing country providing the export credit (which must postpone alternative investments in consequence), the more difficult it is to obtain such finance from existing sources, and the higher the cost of such finance as is available.

4. Other existing sources of such export credit include national export credit institutions and certain regional organizations such as the Inter-American Development Bank, which refinances exports of capital goods mostly to other Latin American countries. However, the domestic export finance institutions have been able to provide only for relatively small amounts of financing and the regional organizations have involved themselves in such activities to a limited extent. At the regional level, the Latin American countries established BLADEX (the Latin American Export Bank) in 1979, which focuses on the

stimulation of export credit for non-traditional exports. Its scale of operations has increased rapidly, but it appears still to fall short of needs. The recently established Asean Finance Corporation may engage in export financing, but this activity will have to compete with many other credit needs the Corporation intends to meet. Some countries have established mechanisms for export credit insurance, which assist the individual exporter to discount export paper in the capital markets and thus realize the foreign exchange, but the small volume of such business and the lack of trained staff, among other reasons, have limited such operations to a very small scale to date.

The scale of requirements

5. Although it is extremely difficult to make forecasts of the potential development of non-traditional exports from developing countries, some estimates made by the UNCTAD secretariat for a limited range of capital and manufactured goods which might require medium- and longer-term export credits suggest a total of such exports of about $29 billion in 1980; at a conservative growth rate of 20 per cent p.a. (actual growth over 1970–80 was 33 per cent p.a., both in current prices), this leads to a level of non-traditional exports of $71 billion in 1985. Although a significant proportion of this trade is currently constituted by intra-firm transfers (some estimates ranging up to fully one-half), and for the rest a certain amount of the necessary finance could be made available by domestic institutions and by international commercial banks and other sources, it nevertheless seems clear that the existing facilities for the provision of export finance are unlikely to prove adequate to supply sufficient resources to meet the increased credit needs which would be associated with such growth in non-traditional trade, even at commercial rates.

6. It is even more difficult to forecast requirements for the second component of trade requiring additional export finance, namely, the traditional exports to non-traditional markets. Traditional exports by the developing countries amounted to about $113 billion in 1980 and they are expected to grow at about 11–12 per cent p.a. in current prices to 1985, when they would total nearly $195 billion. The growth in future export

credit needs from this component could therefore be substantial. In order to provide a very rough estimate, it has been assumed for the purposes of this chapter that the expansion of non-traditional markets would take place largely within the South, where it is clear that needs for export credit are the greatest. The focus has therefore been on the growth in South–South trade in traditional products, which are expected to more than double between 1980 and 1985, from $24 billion to $49 billion.

A new facility

7. Any approach to palliating this potential credit shortfall at the international level would need to focus on two specific areas:

(a) financing and refinancing of export credit; and
(b) export credit guarantees.

The direct provision of finance/refinance for export credit is straightforward, but it is clearly more capital-intensive than export credit guarantees. The latter, however, can stimulate the provision of export finance since paper guaranteed by an international guarantee facility can be discounted more readily with international banks than paper not carrying such guarantees. Furthermore, an international facility, by carefully selecting and arranging for the 'packaging' of the paper it guarantees (thereby increasing the size of the transactions offered to financiers) should be able to reduce substantially both the level and variance of the credit risks perceived by the ultimate lender of the funds and thus obtain finer terms in the financial markets. It should also be able to transcend the 'country limits' imposed by the international banks, since they will tend to look to the facility as the primary obligator, even though it is technically only a guarantor. All of these factors should enable such a facility both to stimulate a greater flow of commercial export credit, particularly to the non-traditional sector (whether this be products or markets), and to reduce the costs associated with such credits.

8. Nevertheless, although an international guarantee facility has been under discussion in UNCTAD for several years now, there has been little progress towards establishing it, primarily because

the industrial countries have had difficulty in agreeing to participate in it. Studies undertaken in connection with UNCTAD's proposed North–South facility have, however, indicated considerable interest in it on the part of private banks (unsurprisingly in view of the fact that such 'trade finance' is covered in most cases by goods produced and already sold); indeed the BLADEX success is due in part to its appeal to commercial bank interests. A South–South investment guarantee facility would therefore be likely to attract private bank funds also. It should be added that not all needs are likely to be met by a guarantee facility: some exports will require finance/refinance, particularly those of the poorer countries' exporters. Hence, a combination of export finance, refinance and guarantee mechanisms is needed, operating most likely under one umbrella.

9. A further issue is the need for some form of subsidization for the export finance provided by any new facility, or by existing ones. As noted earlier, the industrial countries offer heavily subsidized credit terms to qualifying exports (the current interest rates ranging around 10 per cent p.a.). Moreover, they frequently combine aid funds with such subsidized credits, resulting in even softer average terms. A South–South facility for export credit finance, refinance and guarantees could be implemented on a strictly commercial basis (as, for example, is the case of BLADEX, which, as a supplier of finance and guarantees, is projected to earn more than a 30 per cent return on subscribed capital by its fifth year of operation). But equally, relatively small amounts of grant or concessional finance could enable significant subsidization of the terms offered in the direct finance/refinance, and/or guarantee areas, thus reinforcing the basic competitiveness of developing country exporters. In order to ensure the commercial integrity of the facility, however, any such subsidization should be viewed as entirely separate from the basic functions of the facility. This could best be achieved if a separate interest account were created within the facility, which would be charged with any subsidies provided. Such a subsidy account would clearly need a separate source of funds—presumably grants from interested participants.

Possible capital requirements

10. Assuming that 30 per cent of total new financing requirements would be accounted for by intra-firm trade or financed by various existing facilities, with the proposed facility providing direct finance/refinance for 20 per cent, and guarantees for the remainder, Annexe 5.1 works out a capital structure to meet these requirements for new finance/guarantees for both traditional and non-traditional exports. The calculations show that the facility would require total access to capital for the initial three years (1983–5) of $8.7 billion for finance/refinance and $21.7 billion for guarantees, if a 100 per cent capital cover were required of all guarantees. Various studies suggest that such cover could be as low as 10 per cent without serious risk, but for the sake of conservatism, a 25 per cent cover has been assumed here. This leads to a total capital requirement for guarantees of $5.4 billion for the three years.

11. These calculations require, however, some qualification. Thus, should the role particularly of TNCs diminish in relative terms in future trading arrangements, it is likely that traditional exports would require additional export credit financing. Additional finance would also be required should the share of capital goods in non-traditional exports expand substantially, because of the longer credit period associated with such products. On the other hand, the capital cover assumed above for the guarantee activity of the proposed institution is extremely conservative, and might be reduced by a factor of two or three without impairing the financial soundness of the scheme, thus increasing substantially the potential scale of the guarantees provided by the facility. Moreover, because of the revolving nature of trade finance and its commercial attractiveness, a given commitment of equity by participants in the proposed facility will tend over time to support a much higher volume of export credit finance, as outside lenders translate a proven 'track record' into a higher gearing ratio (private commercial banks often have gearing ratios of 25:1 or more). It is thus not likely that equity commitment for the finance/refinance activity of the proposed facility would need to increase greatly over that which might initially be accepted. On the whole, therefore, the capital structure suggested above would seem to be adequate for several years at least, particularly when allowance

is made for the future expansion of the activities of the IDB facility, BLADEX lending, and Asean Finance Corporation export finance.

Conclusions

12. The highly profitable experience of hundreds of private commercial banks in providing finance or refinance for export credits, the success of BLADEX in Latin America, and the interest expressed by private financial institutions in an international facility to guarantee export credit paper, all combine to suggest strongly that the proposed facility, if it applied strictly commercial criteria to its credit risk analysis, would both succeed as a commercially viable operation, and attract the participation of private financiers. This being the case, it would seem appropriate to consider treating such a facility as a commercial joint venture between national export credit institutions or central banks in the exporting developing countries, and public and private capital from outside these countries. If this were done, the facility could logically become a department or window of the proposed South Bank, the joint venture institution.

13. Commercial terms would not, of course, be appropriate for all of the finance/guarantees provided by this department of the proposed joint venture institution. However, as indicated earlier, it would seem necessary and also logical, that any subsidization of terms, whether for finance or guarantees, should be provided for from a quite separate interest subsidy account of the joint venture institution, an account which conceivably could have much broader purposes than merely the subsidization of export credits. What is important, indeed essential, however, is that such an account, presumably financed by grants from interested parties, be kept strictly separate from the coldly commercial assessment of credit risks in the finance/guarantee department of the proposed South–South joint venture institution. Only in this way will commercial credibility be maintained, and the participation in the proposed institution of private finance companies ensured.

Annexe 5.1 Capital requirements of proposed facility

A. Export projections

Assumptions

1. Average annual growth rate (in nominal terms of *non-traditional* exports by developing countries over period 1980–5 is 20 per cent.

2. Average annual growth rate (in nominal terms) of *traditional* exports by developing countries over period 1980–5 is 11.4 per cent.

3. Share of South–South trade in traditional exports expands by 3.2 per cent p.a.

Table A.1 Projected exports of developing countries ($ billion)

	1980	1981	1982	1983	1984	1985
Total non-traditional exports	36.7	44.0	52.8	63.3	76.1	91.3
financed by MT credit	8.0	9.6	11.5	13.8	16.6	19.9
financed by LT credit	28.7	34.4	41.3	49.5	59.5	71.4
Total traditional exports	113.3	127.3	142.5	158.7	176.1	194.4
South–South	24.2	28.1	32.5	37.3	42.8	48.8

B. Export credit projections

Assumptions

1. Eighty per cent of the *increase* in total non-traditional and South–South traditional exports over the levels reached in 1982 is eligible for coverage by the proposed facility.

2. Of the amount specified in (1) above, 20 per cent is eligible for *finance/refinance* and 50 per cent for *guarantee* by the proposed facility.

3. South–South trade in traditional exports is eligible for short-term (ST) credit only.

4. Average lengths of maturity of credits is as follows:

(i) ST: 3 months (ii) MT: 7.5 months (iii) LT: 36 months

5. LT credits are repaid in equal annual instalments.

6. Annualized credit requirement for ST and MT credits for each year is obtained from the formula: $\frac{\text{exports} \times \text{maturity}}{12}$.

Table A.2 Projected export credit requirements of developing countries ($ billion)

1983	1983	1984	1985
I. Increase in exports relative to 1982:			
A. South–South traditional (ST credit)	4.8	10.3	16.3
B. Non-traditional, of which:			
MT credit	2.3	5.1	8.4
LT credit	8.2	18.2	30.1
II. Annualized credit requirements[1] eligible for coverage by facility in form of:			
A. Finance, of which:			
ST credit[2]	0.19	0.41	0.65
MT credit[3]	0.23	0.51	0.84
LT credit[4]	1.31	2.91	4.82
B. Guarantees, of which:			
ST credit[5]	0.48	1.03	1.63
MT credit[6]	0.58	1.28	2.10
LT credit[7]	3.30	7.28	12.00
III. Outstanding credit covered by facility in form of:			
A. Finance, of which:			
ST plus MT credit	0.42	0.92	1.49
LT credit[8]	1.31	3.78	7.20
B. Guarantees, of which:			
ST plus MT credit	1.06	2.31	3.73
LT credit[8]	3.30	12.52	17.95

Table A.2 (*cont.*)

Notes

1. Weighted by maturity
2. $.2 \times .8 \times \frac{3}{12} = .04$
3. $.2 \times .8 \times \frac{7.5}{12} = .10$
4. $.2 \times .8 = .16$
5. $.5 \times .8 \times \frac{3}{12} = .10$
6. $.5 \times .8 \times \frac{7.5}{12} = .25$
7. $.5 \times .8 = .40$

(Notes 2–7: Figures obtained by applying these factors to the corresponding export figures)

8. Assuming each year's credit repaid in equal instalments of 1/3 each.

C. Projected capital requirements

Assumptions

1. In respect of *guarantees*, the proposed facility would maintain a 25 per cent reserve against liabilities.

2. In respect of *finance/refinance*, no profits are allocated to reduce outstanding borrowings by the proposed facility.

Table A.3 Projected cumulative requirements of access to capital ($ billion)

	1983	1984	1985
Finance/refinance	1.7	4.7	8.7
Guarantees	1.1	3.7	5.4
Total	2.8	8.4	14.1

6 ENERGY INVESTMENT

F. ABBATE

The problem

1. The use of energy in the world is grossly unbalanced, as it reflects world income distribution. The consumption of energy per head in industrialized countries compared to middle-income and low-income countries is in the proportion of 100:10:1. The oil-importing developing countries (OIDCs) obtain about half of their commercial energy from oil and in 1980 they spent US $74 billion on importing oil. In some countries like Brazil, Turkey and India, oil imports now absorb over 50 per cent of export earnings. The OIDCs' energy consumption is expected to rise from 14 million barrels per day of oil equivalent (mbdoe) in 1980 to 24 million mbdoe by 1990, even to meet modest GNP growth objectives and assuming a rigorous programme of energy conservation. Domestic energy production in OIDCs needs to be maximized between now and the end of the decade for these countries to reduce their oil deficits to substainable levels relative to GNP while achieving acceptable rates of economic growth.

Investment requirements

2. The total investment needed for an expanded energy programme in OIDCs has been estimated by the World Bank at $450 to $500 billion (in 1980 dollars) over the next decade, or at $45–50 billion per year, as compared to less than $20 billion per year over the past five years. The true shortage facing such countries is not one of energy resources but of capital. Given the staggering size of the financial needs for energy investment, the whole issue becomes a North–South concern, rather than South–South. On oil, gas and coal alone, the requirements are expected to be around $75 billion

(Table 1), while investments in electric power would amount to some $340 billion.

Table 1 OIDCs' investment requirements in oil, gas and coal, 1981–1990 (in 1980 US $ billion)

Oil	41.0
Exploration	12.5
Development	28.5
Gas	22.0
Coal	11.5
Total	74.5

Source: World Bank, 'Energy in the developing Countries', August 1980, p. 7.

Sources of finance

3. In the recent past, one-third of the overall capital requirements for OIDCs' energy investment was derived from external financing. Eighty per cent of the external financing was represented by private capital and the remaining 20 per cent from official sources. While electric power has long attracted a substantial flow of capital from both public and private sources, especially suppliers' credits, there has been little external financing of coal, which is likely to be one of the main sources of additional fuel in the next decades. Although private sources are expected to continue to play the main role in financing oil and gas investment, additional financing from public sources will be required, especially for exploration. The need to finance exploration and development of energy is now increasingly recognized. The international financial institutions are expanding or planning to expand in these fields, but there remain large gaps. The World Bank's current programme for petroleum exploration and development probably represents not more than 7 per cent of the oil importing Third World's investment requirements. Many of the OIDCs may have deposits of significance for their own economies but not for world trade. In many of them, too, private foreign investment may be inhibited by consideration of creditworthiness or other factors.

terms. A mechanism for offering exploration finance on special terms would be an important means of enabling countries to obtain knowledge about their resources, without creating dependence on TNCs. In the past—and still today in a number of places—the oil and mineral companies have justified the claims for relatively high profits by the high risks of failure in exploration, the argument being that high profits from operating oil wells and mines are needed to attract sufficient capital to undertake the uncertain search for oil and minerals. It follows that, if the international community undertakes the task or assumes the risk, through a public body, of oil and minerals exploration, there would be less need for claiming the higher-than-average profits in the exploitation of successful ventures. Financing of oil exploration is discussed in greater detail in Annexe 6. 1.

A new energy facility

5. Following the failure of past energy initiatives, such as the energy affiliate of the World Bank, there is a strong argument in favour of a new energy facility dealing only with oil, gas and coal and, perhaps, new sources of energy, while leaving the financing of electric power to existing IFIs and private sources. The energy affiliate proposed by the World Bank would have entailed for 1982–6 the taking-over of the then 'current' World Bank energy programme amounting to $10.7 billion (in 1980 prices) and additional lending of some $12.4 billion of which roughly $5.5 billion would account for oil, gas and coal (Table 2). If a new energy facility were created, it could concentrate on such 'additional' lending of $1.1 billion per year for oil, gas and coal, or $11 billion over the decade 1982–91. This facility could also establish a special 'window' to operate the $1 billion Exploration Insurance Fund proposed in Annexe 6.1. On the whole, the facility would have to mobilize financial resources amounting to $12 billion, which would cover some 16 per cent of OIDCs' investment requirements. If such a facility were to finance, on average, one-third of the project cost, its financing would be associated to projects totalling $36 billion, or about half of overall requirements.

Table 2 Desirable multilateral lending for oil, gas and coal additional to World Bank present programme, 1982–6 (in US $ billion)

	Current $	1980 $
Oil and gas	5.8	4.5
Exploration	1.8	1.4
Development	4.0	3.1
Coal	1.4	1.0
Total	7.2	5.5

Source: World Bank.

Capital structure of an energy facility

6. An energy facility with universal membership and with financial needs of around $12 billion could be structured along the following lines.

Table 3 Capital structure of the proposed energy facility (in 1980 US $)

	Lending window	Insurance fund	Total
Paid-in capital	500	1,000	1,500
(OIDCs and OPEC)	(250)	(500)	(750)
(Developed countries)	(250)	(500)	(750)
Callable capital	5,000	–	5,000
(OIDCs and OPEC)	(2,500)	–	(2,500)
(Developed countries)	(2,500)	–	(2,500)
Total capital	5,500	1,000	6,500
(OIDCs and OPEC)	(2,750)	(500)	(3,250)
(Developed countries)	(2,750)	(500)	(3,250)
Borrowings	10,500	–	10,500
Total loanable funds (Paid-in capital + borrowings)	11,000	1,000	12,000

7. The proposed capital structure is based on the following premises:

(a) a capital base of $6.5 billion which is equally shared between developing countries (OIDCs and OPEC together) and developed countries;
(b) such capital is divided into $1.5 billion paid-in capital (of which $500 million for lending and $1 billion for insurance purposes) and $5 billion callable capital, as a guarantee for market borrowings to be raised by the lending 'window' of the facility;
(c) a capital lending ratio, or gearing ratio, for the lending window of 2:1. Such a ratio, although twice as high as the extremely conservative IBRD's gearing ratio, can still be regarded as prudent, and thus acceptable to capital markets;
(d) cash outlays in form of paid-in capital would be modest as the $500 million needed for lending purposes could be disbursed over three years, say $160 million per year, while the $1 billion needed for the Insurance Fund might be called in over a ten-year period starting from the fourth year of operations (see Annexe 6. 1);
(e) lending by the facility would be on non-concessional terms. An element of concessionality can be introduced only with the provision of a greater amount of paid-in capital or a special interest subsidy account. Concessional terms would be needed for projects in the least developed countries, for exploration and for funding feasibility studies for new and renewable sources of energy, the latter as proposed by the Group of 77 at the Nairobi Conference.

8. Finally, it would be recalled that the scope of the proposed energy facility is limited and much greater concerted effort by the international community would be required for it to play an important role in the financing of OIDCs' energy investment. This would also involve an expanded energy lending, especially for electric power, by the World Bank, regional development banks and the OPEC Fund, as well as any further South–South initiative that might emerge in the context of joint ventures among developing countries.

Voting structure

9. The voting structure of the energy facility would have to reflect the general principle of equality of votes of all developing countries and all developed countries. For the purpose of voting distribution, OPEC countries and OIDCs could be grouped together, like in the Common Fund, or separately, as in the case of IFAD. The voting structure as well as capital contributions could be revised periodically, to take into account changes in the relative financial strength of member countries, as well as their relative importance as lenders to the institution. As an example, every five years there could be a redistribution of a certain percentage, say 25 per cent, of capital and votes among groups to reflect these factors.

Annexe 6.1 The financing of oil exploration in OIDCs

Introduction

1. Predicting where undiscovered oil reserves lie is still a highly uncertain business. The only sure way to find out is to drill exploratory wells. But drilling is expensive, complicated and risky. This is one reason why only 2–4 per cent of current world exploration is taking place in OIDCs, where the ratio of proven reserves to remaining ultimate recoverable oil reserves (14 per cent) is much below the current world rate of about 37 per cent. A second reason is that few of such countries harbour fields which are large enough to make a dent in the needs of an industrialized country. Most future discoveries are expected to be better suited to import subsitution than to filling the multinationals' needs for crude supplies. Still, the potential exists for many small- to medium-size fields.

Sources of finance

2. On average, worldwide, the number of exploratory wells that discover petroleum is about 10 per cent of the total number of wells drilled, though this ratio may rise to 20–30 per cent in especially favourable areas. Accordingly, it is difficult, if not virtually impossible, to secure funds for exploration from banks or other financial institutions which are concerned with securing

a relatively safe return on their investment. Commercial banks are increasingly willing to extend 'project financing' to the safer oil development activities, but project financing cannot be arranged for exploration.

3. Oil exploration has been traditionally financed by risk capital invested by multinational oil companies. Unlike individual countries, multinational companies are able to compensate for the loss resulting from any particular venture with gains in other ventures throughout the world. The bargaining power of multinational companies derives in part from this built-in insurance mechanism and is reflected in the high risk premium being paid by host countries in terms of their reduced share of benefits from oil exploitation.

4. Relatively few developing countries appear to be in a position to finance petroleum exploration entirely, or even largely from internal funds. In a few particularly favoured nations (Brazil, Mexico), the large prospective areas, the surpluses generated by past oil production, or simply the general health of the economy, may permit the funding of petroleum exploration. For most of the OIDCs, however, it appears that the financial requirements of exploration, coupled with the high risks involved, make internal financing unlikely. In the absence of alternative sources of finance, these countries have been relying on foreign oil companies for financing exploration.

The role of multilateral institutions

5. Multilateral financing for petroleum exploration has been extremely limited. Despite significant efforts made by UNDP as a source of funds for exploration of natural resources, the bulk of its financing, including that provided through the Revolving Fund for Natural Resources Exploration, has been in the sector of non-fuel minerals. Early in 1980, an attempt was made by the UNDP to establish an Energy Fund for the financing of pre-drilling survey works with administrative arrangements similar to those of the Revolving Fund. The Energy Fund's expenditures on petroleum surveys would be recovered at least partially from the proceeds of the sales of findings to the oil companies. The UNDP Governing Council, however, did not

take any action on this proposal and only authorized the Administrator to seek and accept voluntary contributions for an Energy Account to finance pre-investment activities in the energy field.

6. Among the international financial institutions, the World Bank is by far the largest source of oil exploration finance. Assistance to petroleum development began in 1977, and in 1979 an accelerated programme was approved which included for the first time financing for exploration activities. Lending by the Bank for oil and gas has grown rapidly from one $150 million project in fiscal 1977 to twelve projects for a total of about $650 million in loans during fiscal 1981. Although about half of these loans were specifically directed at exploration, the Bank's emphasis has been on pre-drilling activities, such as seismic and geophysical surveys which are normally inexpensive as compared to the capital intensive, high risk exploratory drilling. Under the guidance of its Executive Directors, who have stressed the need for caution in providing finance in support of exploration activities, the Bank has so far financed only a handful of projects including exploratory drilling.

7. The OPEC Fund for International Development has become, to a great extent, an energy fund, as it gives priority in its project financing to the energy sector. But the $370 million energy projects so far financed by the OPEC Fund have concentrated on energy development, rather than exploration.

The need for new initiatives

8. As shown above, while multilateral institutions have recently recognized the urgent need for OIDCs to search for petroleum deposits and have offered to assist them in this effort, the actual assistance offered so far for drilling exploration has been minute and in the form of loans to be repaid by the recipient government with interest, even if the outcome is complete failure.

9. The financial risk of drilling exploration remains the crucial issue facing OIDCs. There seems to be a need for new financing arrangements for petroleum exploration in order to replace or

supplement those offered by petroleum companies, or at least to underwrite the normal risks involved in such exploration and thus eliminate or reduce the highly inflated premium placed by the foreign companies on such a risk.

10. In this connection, an interesting proposal has been recently put forward by the International Energy Development Corporation (IEDC). The essence of the proposal is the setting-up of an Exploration Insurance Fund which would operate as follows:

(a) the Fund provides insurance coverage against failure to find oil or gas on an exploratory programme previously approved by the Fund and financed either by foreign risk capital or a national oil company;
(b) the insurance coverage is provided without payment of any premium, but should there be a commercial discovery, the insured oil company would be required to replenish the Fund by making payments from the proceeds of oil production. Such payments would be determined by a 'payback ratio', that is, a multiple of the amount insured, such a multiple being established on actuarial principles;
(c) in order to avoid the exhaustion of the Fund's resources before success is experienced, the Fund's capital base has to be strong enough to withstand a number of consecutive failures. Its financial requirements are estimated at \$500 million to \$1 billion spread over a period of ten years. This would allow the Fund to provide, say, 75 per cent coverage on between thirteen and twenty-seven exploration programmes of an average cost of \$50 million each;
(d) OPEC and OECD countries would be expected to provide the required capital; loan financing from commercial banks might also be envisaged. However, this would call for the Fund to become a profit-making institution by increasing the payments from successful explorations.

11. The proposed scheme appears to offer several advantages:

(a) While the Fund in itself would not provide any finance, credible insurance coverage of exploration risks would make exploration for the first time a bankable proposition. Thus, exploration could be financed on a project basis by commercial banks. Financing by commercial banks would increase the flow of exploration funds available either to national oil companies or foreign firms. With the same amount of risk capital, these institutions could undertake a much larger number of exploration programmes by matching their capital with commercial bank loans. If, for example, the Fund were to offer a 75 per cent insurance coverage, a national oil company would be able to spread its $50 million capital over exploration programmes totalling $200 million by attracting $150 million loan financing.

(b) The Fund should be able to increase the flow of exploration funds not only from the large multinational oil companies but also from the smaller 'independent' private firms, by providing a vehicle which would permit them to diversify risks. In case of successful exploration, the foreign company would have to accept that its rewards are scaled down to take account of the lower degree of risks borne by the company. In each case, the host government should not be in any less advantageous revenue position than it would have been without the insurance coverage for the company. With a reduction of exploration risks, the host government should be in a much stronger position to negotiate a more equitable sharing of the economic rent deriving from petroleum exploitation.

(c) The financial requirements of the Fund are relatively small amounting to about $50 million to $100 million per year of funds committed, but not necessarily disbursed. The first payment would not be required until about three years after the Fund is set up. Ultimately, the Fund would be self-sustaining.

Conclusions

12. The Exploration Insurance Fund scheme as proposed by IEDC has been presented to a number of international seminars, including the United Nations Seminar on Petroleum Exploration Strategies, and has been received with great interest by potential beneficiaries as well as by potential providers of funds.

13. If the proposal attracts broad support by the international financial community, it would need further elaboration, especially with regard to the size of its capital and replenishment

charges. Prima facie, it would seem prudent to start with a strong capital base of $1 billion, rather than the proposed lower limit of $500 million. As explained in 10(c) above, the facility's capital of $1 billion would support twenty-seven exploration programmes. With one chance out of ten of success, the probability of at least one successful programme out of twenty-seven is 94 per cent. Alternatively, a $500 million capital could finance only thirteen programmes and the probability of at least one success would be reduced to 75 per cent.

14. Another critical parameter for the financial viability of the scheme is the size of replenishment charges, or the payback ratio to be applied to successful exploration programmes. Too low a ratio would jeopardize the Fund's ability to be self-sustaining. Too high a ratio would have adverse effects on the Fund's capacity to attract a large number of clients with good-grade acreage. As an example, if a $1 billion Fund chose a payback ratio of fifteen, the probability of its self-sustainment (i.e. of two or more successful programmes) would be 75 per cent. Such probability would decline to 50 per cent, if the payback ratio were reduced to ten.

7 EXPORT FINANCING IN DEVELOPING COUNTRIES

A. TRAN-NGUYEN

I Introduction

1. It is often recognized that one of the most efficient measures to assist developing countries in their efforts to increase exports is the provision of adequate financial resources to the export sector. In fact, export credit, at both the pre-shipment and post-shipment levels, is an important element in export promotion policies, especially when new products and new markets are involved. It is often found that exporters of non-traditional goods or of goods destined to new importing markets do not have an easy access to financial resources, without governmental support.

2. For purposes of analysis it is convenient to classify exports from developing countries into two broad categories: traditional and non-traditional exports. Export credit associated with each of these two categories of exports may differ with respect to its terms and to the way in which it is financed. Although traditional and non-traditional exports may not necessarily be the same for every country, the definition used here may be applied to the great majority of developing countries. Traditional exports encompass exports of primary agricultural and mineral products and products with a minor degree of industrial transformation, while non-traditional exports include exports of manufactured products (consumer and intermediate goods), capital goods and services. Exports of different categories of goods from developing countries are reported in Tables 1, 2, 3 and 4. Non-traditional exports may generally be classified as exports of manufactured goods[1] as defined in the UNCTAD Handbook of International Trade and Development Statistics.

3. Exports from developing countries have been increasing

Table 1 Exports from developing countries and territories

	US $ million							Average annual rate of growth (per cent)	
	1960	1969	1970	1973	1977	1978	1979	1960–9	1970–9
Total exports:[a]									
– to world	27,390	48,880	54,980	108,790	288,477	300,802	416,609	6.64	25.23
– to total developing countries	6,100	9,820	10,970	21,410	68,676	73,342	103,185	5.43	28.28
All food items:[b]									
– to world	9,210	12,750	14,570	23,140	48,235	49,361	57,861	3.68	16.56
– to total developing countries	1,680	2,210	2,330	4,020	9,232	9,901	15,554	3.09	23.48
Agricultural raw materials:[c]									
– to world	5,000	5,490	5,500	10,100	12,349	14,373	19,515	1.04	15.11
– to total developing countries	170	235	250	265	3,315	3,798	5,391	3.66	40.66

Fuels:[d]									
– to world	7,650	16,210	18,100	43,040	164,216	158,954	235,747	8.7	33.00
– to total developing countries	2,270	3,360	3,780	7,540	36,410	35,499	48,641	4.45	32.82
Ores and metals:[e]									
– to world	2,978	6,390	7,400	9,600	14,603	16,314	21,935	8.85	12.83
– to total developing countries	186	515	720	1,160	2,830	3,408	5,043	12.39	24.14
Manufactured goods:[f]									
– to world	2,440	7,750	9,170	21,810	48,087	60,462	79,182	13.70	27.06
– to total developing countries	1,030	2,650	3,050	5,980	16,622	20,539	27,729	11.07	27.79

Source: UNCTAD, Handbook of International Trade and Development Statistics, several issues.

Notes: [a] SITC (0 to 9)
[b] SITC (0 + 1 + 22 + 4)
[c] SITC (2 – (22 + 27 + 28))
[d] SITC (3)
[e] SITC (27 + 28 + 67 + 68)
[f] SITC (5 + 6 + 7 + 8 – (67 + 68))

Table 2 Exports from developing countries of Latin America

	US $ million							Average annual rate of growth (per cent)	
	1960	1969	1970	1973	1977	1978	1979	1960–9	1970–9
Total exports:[a]									
– to world	10,170	15,440	17,430	29,060	60,902	64,856	85,378	4.75	19.31
– to total developing countries	1,860	3,120	3,450	5,070	15,122	15,765	22,760	5.91	23.32
– to Latin America	1,680	2,830	3,120	4,110	12,233	12,589	18,733	5.96	22.04
All food items:[b]									
– to world	4,330	6,050	7,160	11,470	24,112	24,777	28,604	3.78	16.63
– to total developing countries	390	660	700	1,470	3,401	3,409	4,613	6.02	23.30
– to Latin America	305	530	550	860	1,903	2,104	3,101	6.33	21.19
Agricultural raw materials:[c]									
– to world	976	1,210	1,100	1,430	2,078	2,911	3,038	2.48	12.07

– to total developing countries	100	225	270	315	511	639	833	9.43	13.33
– to Latin America	95	170	195	165	268	373	556	6.68	12.35
Fuels:[d]									
– to world	3,240	4,030	4,150	7,980	20,138	20,239	30,506	2.45	24.81
– to total developing countries	1,230	1,430	1,490	1,300	6,187	5,988	8,995	1.69	22.11
– to Latin America	1,150	1,350	1,440	1,240	5,617	5,288	8,073	1.80	21.11
Ores and metals:[e]									
– to world	1,310	2,690	3,215	3,670	5,992	6,652	9,445	8.32	12.72
– to total developing countries	41	204	261	379	1,047	1,159	1,976	19.51	25.22
– to Latin America	37	196	242	351	933	989	1,671	20.35	23.95
Manufactured goods:[f]									
– to world	298	1,430	1,750	4,020	8,398	9,981	13,327	19.03	25.30
– to total developing countries	85	585	700	1,435	3,883	4,498	6,184	23.90	27.38
– to Latin America	66	570	670	1,315	3,478	3,808	5,252	29.37	25.71

Source: UNCTAD, Handbook of International Trade and Development Statistics, several issues.
Notes: see Table 1.

Table 3 Exports from developing countries of Africa

	US $ million							Average annual rate of growth (per cent)	
	1960	1969	1970	1973	1977	1978	1979	1960–9	1970–9
Total exports:[a]									
– to world	5,310	10,980	12,310	20,360	47,762	44,057	66,576	8.40	20.63
– to total developing countries	680	1,060	1,240	2,260	6,599	5,932	7,283	5.05	21.74
– to Africa	350	560	650	860	2,046	1,837	2,900	5.36	18.07
All food items:[b]									
– to world	2,380	3,180	3,570	4,890	8,950	8,538	9,796	3.27	11.87
– to total developing countries	340	395	410	610	880	919	1,256	1.68	13.46
– to Africa	225	230	270	330	561	563	683	0.24	10.86
Agricultural raw materials:[c]									
– to world	1,270	1,250	1,420	2,080	2,385	2,190	2,987	–0.17	8.61

– to total developing countries	150	155	180	260	255	225	431	0.36	10.19
– to Africa	23	38	46	55	73	66	180	5.74	16.37
Fuels:[d]									
– to world	245	3,410	4,060	8,900	30,794	27,464	45,496	34.00	30.80
– to total developing countries	14	205	305	910	4,436	3,747	3,945	34.74	32.90
– to Africa	10	87	96	235	678	490	934	27.17	28.76
Ores and metals:[e]									
– to world	1,058	2,289	2,391	3,021	3,502	3,488	4,181	8.95	6.40
– to total developing countries	57	71	96	203	522	504	308	2.47	13.83
– to Africa	7	23	37	52	379	366	129	14.13	14.88
Manufactured goods:[f]									
– to world	328	810	843	1,389	1,961	2,211	3,998	10.56	18.88
– to total developing countries	96	228	246	271	474	508	1,330	10.09	20.62
– to Africa	61	180	203	183	330	325	964	12.77	18.90

Source: UNCTAD Handbook of International Trade and Development Statistics, several issues.
Notes: See Table 1.

Table 4 Exports from developing countries of Asia (West Asia and South and South-East Asia)

	US $ million							Average annual rate of growth (per cent)	
	1960	1969	1970	1973	1977	1978	1979	1960–9	1970–9
Total exports:[a]									
– to world	11,910	22,090	24,760	58,330	178,369	190,421	262,815	7.10	30.31
– to total developing countries	3,560	5,630	6,260	14,000	46,846	51,544	72,985	5.22	31.37
– to Asia	2,905	4,570	4,955	10,940	33,202	38,847	54,847	5.16	30.62
All food items:[b]									
– to world	2,500	3,330	3,660	6,450	14,430	15,202	18,561	3.23	19.77
– to total developing countries	927	1,145	1,210	1,925	4,894	5,499	9,595	2.37	25.87
– to Asia	745	1,033	1,072	1,756	4,279	4,742	6,158	3.70	21.44
Agricultural raw materials:[c]									
– to world	2,775	3,000	2,925	6,570	7,880	9,279	13,746	0.87	18.76

– to total developing countries	618	655	629	1,800	2,564	2,961	4,230	0.64	23.58
– to Asia	542	557	531	1,594	2,271	2,640	3,765	0.30	24.31
Fuels:[d]									
– to world	4,180	8,760	9,890	26,160	113,278	111,208	159,701	8.57	36.22
– to total developing countries	1,025	1,715	1,990	5,340	25,787	25,749	35,686	5.88	37.81
– to Asia	784	1,296	1,462	3,484	15,515	17,055	25,461	5.74	37.36
Ores and metals:[e]									
– to world	610	1,261	1,523	2,346	4,179	5,273	6,743	8.40	17.97
– to total developing countries	89	241	296	566	1,053	1,528	2,294	11.70	25.55
– to Asia	77	211	267	509	952	1,419	2,146	11.85	26.05
Manufactured goods:[f]									
– to world	1,815	5,514	6,571	16,500	37,708	48,350	62,309	13.14	28.39
– to total developing countries	853	1,818	2,101	4,285	12,290	15,599	20,534	8.77	28.82
– to Asia	643	1,448	1,583	3,509	9,962	12,695	16,903	9.44	30.10

Source: UNCTAD, Handbook of International Trade and Development Statistics, several issues.
Notes: See Table 1.

rapidly, particularly in the last decade. Manufactured exports are growing faster than other exports, with the exception of fuels. The major part of the exports go to developed country markets (see Table 5), although in the case of manufactured goods the proportion going to other developing countries is quite respectable. (For the year 1979, for example, the percentage of total exports from developing countries to developing countries was 24 per cent, while the percentage of manufactured exports is 35 per cent). In addition, it can be seen from Tables 2, 3 and 4 that a large part of exports to developing countries consist of intra-regional trade, particularly in the cases of Latin America and Asia. Thus there is large scope for increasing trade among developing regions. Provision of export credits will then become an essential element in the promotion of trade among developing countries, mainly because the problem of shortage of foreign exchange that most developing countries are facing will induce them to seek deferred payment.

4. The present study will attempt to examine the difficulties encountered by developing countries in the area of export financing and to put forward some proposals to respond to the needs which remain unfilled at the national, regional or international levels. The analysis will focus on post-shipment credit, i.e. at the stage when foreign exchange credits are involved and problems are likely to become critical. This does not imply that all the problems at the pre-shipment level have been solved; they are, however, linked to overall development financing problems.[2]

II Export financing in developed countries

5. Virtually all the economically developed countries today have an efficient and comprehensive system to ensure financial support for exports, especially exports of capital goods, which are sold on a medium- to long-term basis. The export financing system in these countries provides ample financial resources to the exporters, resources which are very often subsidized by their government.

6. The sources of export financing are various and come either

Table 5 Destination of exports from developing countries (per cent)

	World	Developed market economy countries	Socialist countries	Developing countries
1955	100	72.0	2.1	24.9
1960	100	74.4	3.3	20.8
1970	100	72.2	6.9	18.9
1977	100	70.7	3.6	23.8
1978	100	70.6	3.8	24.4
1979	100	71.1	3.2	24.6

Source: UNCTAD, Handbook of International Trade and Development Statistics, several issues.

from the exporting firm, the national banking system, the international capital markets or the government. The domestic banking system assumes, however, a preponderant role in financing, very often with government support in the forms of refinancing facilities at preferential rates or of interest subsidy. Other forms of financing are provided by the forfeiting and factoring markets.

7. International capital markets also constitute an important source of finance and the developed countries, given that they are highly rated by lending institutions, can have easy access to these markets.

8. Increasingly, however, most governments are becoming involved in export financing less in providing direct financing than in reducing the costs and risks associated with such financing. Generally speaking, the government intervenes in business with relatively high risk, that is to say, with longer term maturities and in riskier markets. Government support traditionally takes the form of:

— the provision of refinancing facilities at preferential rates;
— an interest subsidy scheme;
— credit insurance services;

— and, to a much lesser extent, direct official loans to the supplier or to the buyer.

9. Some countries, the best known of which are Belgium and France, are providing, through the Central Bank or another rediscounting institution, refinancing facilities at low cost.

10. Government support through interest subsidy schemes[3] results in substantially insulating the terms of export credits from conditions existing in domestic as well as international markets. The interest rates applied to officially supported export credits are typically lower than those prevailing on money markets for the same maturities. Furthermore, government interest rates are fixed for the whole duration of the loan and they are stable, that is, they do not vary much between old and new loans. Government subsidies are usually given to loans denominated in domestic currency, but more recently these subsidies have been enlarged to Euro-currency loans, because the Euro-currency markets represent a considerable source of export finance. This practice was initiated in 1977 by the British Credit Guarantee Department, which gave insurance cover and guaranteed an agreed rate of return to banks financing export credits at fixed rates in Euro-currencies other than sterling. Other countries, like Italy, are following the British example to grant interest subsidies to Euro-currency export credits.

11. Perhaps the most widely used instrument of government support is the export credit insurance. In practically all developed countries the government has set up corporations or a ministry department to give insurance cover to export credits, in order to facilitate the access of exports to source of finance or to reduce the costs of financing. Export credit insurance is not properly a subsidized operation, since in most agencies the premium charges cover all the expenses and occasional losses are normally covered by accumulated reserves. However, export credit insurance agencies depend on government treasuries as insurers of last resort. Government-supported insurance schemes generally assume the higher risk business, which implies longer maturities, new markets, risk of a non-commercial nature, although commercial risk is also usually included. In some

countries, government insurance schemes also cover other events, such as the escalation of cost during the manufacturing period and the exchange risk. Moreover, insurance has been extended to credits denominated in foreign currency. This practice was initiated in 1977 by the United Kingdom, and has been rapidly followed by other countries, such as France, Sweden, Canada, Italy, West Germany and the United States.

12. Finally, the fourth area of government intervention is direct lending, where the government acts as a sole lender or concurrently with commercial banks. In general, government direct loans are used to finance transactions with large value contract and with long-term maturities, involving essentially capital goods, which are sold mainly to developing countries. A recent form of subsidization in this area has evolved with the development of mixed credits, which consist of commercial lending blended with government funds in the form of government aid or development loans to developing countries. These governmental concessional funds are destined to finance essentially down-payment and local costs associated with large projects in developing countries. The result is that the cost of such credit is considerably reduced and the maturity substantially lengthened.

13. In conclusion, the export financing systems of developed countries, benefiting from a strong government support, usually offer the exporter ample financial resources, competitive low-cost financing and insurance against a wide range of commercial and non-commercial risks as well as provision of guarantees to facilitate bank lending.

III Export financing in developing countries

A. Export financing at the national level

14. National export financing systems in developing countries are less comprehensive and financially weaker than those in developed countries. Developing countries in general suffer from many disadvantages. First, a shortage of resources, especially of foreign exchange resources, often impedes the provision of credits to foreign buyers on a medium- or long-term basis.

In addition, it is often found that the level of interest rates in developing countries is usually higher than in developed countries, which necessitates an accordingly sizeable amount of interest subsidies in order to compete with low-cost subsidized credits from developed countries. Finally, the lack of experience is a big handicap in the organization of an efficient banking network and of insurance agencies to provide cover against trade risks and guarantee for bank lending.

15. On the financing side, distinction must be made between traditional and non-traditional exports. Traditional exports generally require short-term financing of up to 180 days and often benefit from well-established channels of financing. Usually these exports are financed by the transnational producing companies, or by the commercial banks, by way of discounting of export bills. However, small exporters or exporters to developing country markets may find difficulty in obtaining adequate financing even for traditional exports. It has been pointed out, for example, that small farmers in some African countries do not even have access to financial resources. In a study on payments arrangements and trade in Eastern and Southern Africa by the IMF staff, it is found that discounting by commercial banks of bills resulting from intra-regional trade is not very frequent.

16. Non-traditional exports, on the other hand, contain more risks in so far as they are usually destined to new markets and require a financing of longer term, from 180 days to five years. The domestic banking sector is often inadequate to cope with problems faced by exporters. Domestic banks are generally oriented towards short-term loans granted by traditional and established clients. The new exporting manufacturing industries are often considered by banks as being risky and not very profitable, especially when importers are other developing countries.

17. Moreover, the ability of developing countries to finance their export credits on international capital markets is rather restricted. Many of them do not have access to these markets. Others are borrowing heavily in the commercial Euro-currency markets and further borrowing of this kind to support new

export financing needs would count against limits of the exporting country utilizing additional borrowings for this purpose.

18. Experience in exporting manufactured products is relatively new in developing countries. Few of them have been capable of organizing a sophisticated system of export financing to support their exporters. Furthermore, insufficient foreign exchange reserves often impede the provision of credits to overseas buyers.

19. Some countries have implemented government-sponsored export financing and export credit insurance schemes, but in most cases these schemes are modest with respect to both the volume of business undertaken and to the maturities covered. In countries where refinancing facilities are set up by the government, but where export credit insurance schemes do not exist, the central banks or other public institutions providing preferential refinancing have full recourse to the commercial banks, which, in turn, require a high collateral from the exporter. This constitutes a major obstacle for exporters of non-traditional goods in obtaining loans from commercial banks.

20. The functions of export credit insurance is to provide security to exporters for their transaction with foreign buyers and to facilitate the access of exporters to financial resources. These functions are performed by providing two basic types of services: first, to the exporter and insurance cover against risks of non-payment by the importer, including commercial and non-commercial risks, and secondly, guarantee cover to the banks against losses that may arise from a default by the exporter. The insurance activities are rather risky and are usually assumed by the government itself or are undertaken with the support of the government. Moreover, the capacity of insurance schemes in developing countries to function on a self-supporting basis in the early stages is considerably reduced by the fact that the volume of business is still relatively small and often uncertain. Furthermore, a shortage of experienced professional staff and lack of information on export credit insurance systems and practices applied in other developing countries and developed countries also constitute an important handicap.

B. Export financing at the regional level

21. Where the capacity to finance exports at the national level is limited, regional facilities may supplement national efforts in mobilizing resources. However, it must be noted that existing regional mechanisms set up for the specific purpose of export financing are very few and are mainly concentrated in the Latin American region. In addition, the size of these mechanisms is modest, as compared to the needs of the regions that they are covering. No regional scheme has been established to deal with the problems of insurance, reinsurance and guarantees, except the Inter-Arab Investment Guarantee Corporation, which among other activities also provides guarantees on export credits resulting from transactions between its member countries.

22. In the Latin American region, as already mentioned, several mechanisms have been implemented at the regional level to provide financing and refinancing facilities to member countries. The first and oldest mechanism is the one operated by the *Inter-American Development Bank*, a mechanism which was created by the Bank in 1963 and whose activities have since been expanded. This mechanism provides refinancing facilities to member countries at a very preferential interest rate (7 per cent in 1980)[4] under two programmes: a short-term programme which refinances export credits of up to 180 days, and a medium-term programme which refinances export credits of more than 180 days. It is now endowed with US $60 million in ordinary capital to fund the medium-term programme and US $4 million to fund the short-term programme; in addition, the Venezuelan authorities have entrusted it with US $50 million to cover both programmes.[5] Exports eligible for refinancing with ordinary capital resources are intra-Latin American exports of capital goods and services and other non-traditional goods and services. Exports eligible for refinancing with Venezuelan Fund resources are capital goods exported to non-Latin American countries and consumer durables exported within, as well as outside, the Latin American region. The major part of exports refinanced by the IDB consisted of intra-regional trade. The countries which have benefited the most from the IDB mechanism are mainly the relatively more advanced Latin American countries (Argentina, Brazil, Mexico, Peru and Jamaica.)

23. In addition to this refinancing mechanism, the IDB also provides technical assistance to member countries in implementing and strengthening their national export credit and export credit insurance mechanisms. The IDB also participated financially in other regional export financing schemes, such as the Latin American Export Bank (BLADEX), and has actively supported the creation of the Latin American bankers acceptance market.

24. The second regional scheme under study is the abovementioned *Latin American Export Bank* (BLADEX). This institution has the status of a private multinational bank, specialized in the promotion of exports of Latin American countries and endowed with a subscribed capital of US $99 million. It started its operations in 1979. It deals only with stockholder banks and virtually functions as a link between participating international banks and local Latin American banks, some of which may not have access to international capital markets. It finances any transaction which will generate foreign exchange, which implies that it also finances imports of capital goods and raw materials for export projects. It mobilizes funds through deposits from government banks, private banks and international development finance institutions (the Inter-American Development Bank and the OPEC Fund) through borrowing on international capital markets and through the sale of acceptances from BLADEX's portfolio (with recourse to BLADEX). It lends through direct advances, acceptances and medium-term loans at market rates plus a margin. Non-traditional exports account for approximately 60 per cent of the transactions financed by BLADEX; about 73 per cent of total financed exports are destined to markets outside the region.

25. The third Latin American export financing scheme is the Andean Trade Financing System (SAFICO), which was created in 1974 by member countries of the Andean Development Corporation (Bolivia, Colombia, Ecuador, Peru and Venezuela). SAFICO finances non-traditional exports of goods and services from the Andean countries, mainly destined to other member countries of the subregion. Credits are granted to the importer for periods of one to five years. However, given the strong demand for export finance, SAFICO is in need of additional resources.

26. Finally, for the Latin American region, mention should be made of the creation of an association of local credit insurers, scheduled to commence functioning during the first semester of 1982. The objective of this association is to permit an exchange of information among local insurers.

27. Outside the Latin American region, other regional mechanisms of export financing hardly exist, except, perhaps, the Islamic Development Bank and the Inter-Arab Investment Guarantee Corporation. The Islamic Development Bank has a trade financing programme which in principle can finance imports and exports, but which in practice has so far been financing mainly essential goods imported by member countries with balance of payments difficulties. This programme in 1980 represented roughly 64 per cent of total financing approved by the Bank.

28. The Inter-Arab Investment Guarantee Corporation started its operation in 1975 with a capital equivalent to US $80.5 million. Its purpose is to provide insurance coverage for Arab investments in member countries against losses resulting from political risks. Investments eligible for its guarantee include direct investments, portfolio investments and medium- and long-term loans. Henceforth it provides guarantee to export credits arising from transactions among member states.

29. There have been discussions and studies made on different proposals of export credit financing and export credit insurance schemes for the Asian region, but so far none has been implemented.

C. Export financing systems in some developing countries

30. Experience in export financing of a few developing countries, on which information is available, will be analysed in this section. There are different degrees of sophistication in the organization of national export financing systems. A first group of countries is at the simplest stage, where finance provided by commercial banks is often limited at the pre-shipment level or, if provided at the post-shipment level, is limited to the very short term; in addition, there is no official refinancing scheme and insurance mechanisms are either non-existent or

have been very recently set up. A second group of countries do have some government support financing mechanisms, in the form either of an export Fund or rediscounting lines with preferential rates (often limited to short-term credits), generally vested in the Central Bank; they also have insurance schemes, whose coverage, however, are limited to pre-shipment credits. Finally, a third group includes a small number of countries which have implemented relatively comprehensive systems to provide both finance and insurance for export credits. Finance can be provided on a long-term basis and insurance is offered against a wide range of risks. These countries are generally relatively industrialized and have exported goods under medium- or long-term credits.

31. However, the problem commonly found in the sample of countries under study is a foreign exchange constraint which somehow restricts the provision of post-shipment export credits. Government support is very often directed towards non-traditional manufactured exports. It is also found that, even where insurance schemes exist, the percentage of exports which have been insured is rather low on average.

32. In *Kenya*, commercial banks, which are mostly foreign banks, provide the finance. Post-shipment credit is limited to ninety days, or may exceptionally be extended to 180 days. There is no rediscounting facility in the Central Bank and an export credit insurance scheme was recently set up in 1981.

33. In *Nigeria*, commercial and merchant banks provide pre-shipment credits to exporters. In addition, the Central Bank lends directly to the Commodity Boards for the purpose of buying agricultural produce the bulk of which is exported. There is no post-shipment credit. There is no official scheme for insurance and guarantee, although the establishment of the Export Credit Guarantee and Insurance Scheme is under consideration.

34. In *Sri Lanka*, commercial banks provide funds to exporters. The Central Bank has refinancing facilities which are limited to pre-shipment credits. Sri Lanka does not export goods which require medium- and long-term credits, therefore, all export

proceeds have to be recovered in 180 days. The Export Credit Insurance Corporation offers guarantees to banks for their pre-shipment credits to exporters, as well as insurance cover to exporters.

35. In the *Philippines*, short-term export finance is provided by commercial banks which, in turn, can have access to short-term rediscounting facilities with preferential rates of the Central Bank. Medium- and long-term post-shipment credits have not been granted. The Philippine Export and Foreign Loan Guarantee Corporation provides pre-shipment guarantee to banks. Recently, in 1981, the Export Credit Corporation, which is owned by the government, has been created to provide direct export credits, financial guarantees (against commercial and political risks, excluding performance guarantees) to banks, and insurance cover (against non-commercial risks) to exporters.

36. In *Zimbabwe*, commercial and merchant banks provide funds to exporters. The Central Bank has a scheme for re-financing on a short-term basis, by means of acceptance credits. Post-shipment medium- or long-term credits are subject to restrictions laid down by the Reserve Bank. The Export Credit Insurance Corporation provides insurance cover to exporters against political risks (which is reinsured with the government) and commercial risks.

37. In *Barbados*, finance is provided by commercial banks. The exchange control rules ordinarily that export proceeds be repatriated within six months. The Central Bank has a short-term rediscounting facility at preferential rates which can only be used by banks during periods of liquidity constraints. The Central Bank's Export Credit Insurance and Guarantee Scheme offers a pre-shipment guarantee to banks on a short-term basis, as well as an insurance cover to exporters for short-term credits.

38. In *Venezuela*, finance is provided by commercial banks and by a government fund called FINEXPO (Fondos de Financiamiento de las Exportaciones). FINEXPO provides direct financing for long-term buyers' export credits (of five years or more) and for supplier credits, through the discounting of export papers, of up to three years. In addition, FINEXPO gives lines

of credit to national and foreign financial institutions. Commercial banks use lines of credit of FINEXPO to discount export papers of up to one year. They also provide financing to exporters out of their own resources. In addition, commercial banks, in conjunction with FINEXPO, provide half of the funds used to finance buyers' credits. On the other hand, the Central Bank does not have any rediscounting facility. On the insurance side, a private company insures against commercial risks for post-shipment export credits of short- and medium-term of up to three years.

39. In *Mexico*, finance is provided by commercial banks and by a specialized governmental fund, FOMEX (Fondo para el Fomento de la Exportaciones de Productos Manufacturos). FOMEX has been set up to encourage exports of manufactured products. It is a trust fund vested in the Central Bank. On the insurance side, FOMEX provides insurance cover against both commercial and political risks; in addition, a private insurance company, COMESEC, which is a consortium of several private companies and one public company, also provides cover against commercial risks.

40. In *Brazil*, commercial banks finance export credit. In addition, a government fund called CACEX (Cartera de Comércio Exterior) also gives medium- and long-term credits, by refinancing national and foreign financial institutions. On the insurance side, there is a scheme of export credit insurance, which operates through the insurance companies for the coverage of commercial risks, under the supervision of the IRB (Instituto de Reseguros do Brazil). The IRB, on behalf of the government, insured against political risks and other commercial risks which have not been covered by private companies.

41. In *Korea*, export finance is provided by commercial banks, the Korea Exchange Bank, and the Export–Import Bank of Korea (EXIM Bank). The Central Bank refinances the commercial banks at a preferential rate for short-term, pre-shipment credit. The EXIM Bank, which is owned by the government, extends only medium- and long-term export credits. On the insurance side, the EXIM Bank, on behalf of the government and using resources of the Export Insurance Fund, provides insurance cover against both commercial and political risks.

42. In *India*, the system of export financing is relatively sophisticated and comparable to those existing in developed countries. On the financing side, commercial banks are the source of export credit. In addition, the newly-established Export–Import Bank, which is owned by the government, provides medium- and long-term credits. On the insurance side, the official Export Credit and Guarantee Corporation provides both guarantees to banks and insurance cover to exporters against a wide range of risks.

IV Conclusion and proposals

43. Two strategies seem to be promising to support developing countries' efforts to bring about a necessary increase in their exports. On the one hand, export earnings can be substantially increased if the structure of exports is more diversified, implying a bigger share of manufactured goods in total exports. This type of diversification will help to increase and stabilize export earnings, in so far as primary products are often income-inelastic and their prices rather unstable. On the other hand, diversification in the export market by intensifying trade between developing countries is possible, given the small percentage of intra-developing country trade in total exports from developing countries.

44. The implementation of these strategies would require that more emphasis should be put on export credit policy. In the first place, international trade of manufactured goods is usually carried out on the basis of credit. Furthermore, in this market developing countries are facing a strong competition from developed countries, which are in general better endowed with financial resources and institutional organization. In the second place, developing countries are generally subject to foreign exchange constraint, which induces them to defer payment of their imports and consequently to require adequate credit from exporters.

45. The problems that developing countries are facing in the financing of their export credit relate to the availability of resources and to the institutional organization. With respect to traditional exports, it is noted that in some countries the

provision of short-term export credit has been adequately handled by commercial banks and export companies. However, in other countries small exporters can hardly have access to financial resources. Intra-developing country trade in general suffers from the difficulty of obtaining finance from commercial banks. Such being the case, it is necessary that the governments concerned adopt measures to support more actively small exporters and new markets by either giving direct financing or refinancing or by giving guarantees to banks in order to mobilize resources for exporters. The implementation of a regional or international facility to finance traditional exports would bring an appreciable support to small and less developed countries which might not have the necessary resources. In addition, the organization of an effective (regional) market for bankers' acceptances would enhance developing countries' access to international capital markets for the purpose of financing their trade. In this respect, mention should be made of efforts to implement the Latin American acceptance market. A proposal to create such a market for the Asean countries has also been under discussion.[6]

46. From the institutional point of view, the export financing systems in many developing countries are far from being adequate and effective. At the financing level, the banking system does not satisfactorily respond to the requirements of exporters because, for instance, banking procedures are rigid, time-consuming and security-oriented. There are, in addition, no refinancing schemes or, if they exist, the same problems occur again. At the insurance level, lack of experience and competent staff, associated sometimes with an insufficient and unstable volume of business and a shortage of credit information, often impedes the implementation of an effective insurance scheme. Finally, the absence of economic information on overseas markets and/or credit information of foreign buyers weighs heavily on the reluctance of exporters to explore new markets and to export new products.

47. In order to fill this institutional gap, technical assistance can be provided by developed countries or more experienced developing countries, by regional development banks (as in the case of the Inter-American Development Bank) or by

international organizations (such as the International Trade Centre). At a further stage it may be envisaged that a regional insurance and reinsurance scheme[7] would be set up to give direct insurance cover to exporters of countries that do not have national schemes, to reinsure exports which have been insured by national schemes, to collect and supply information on buyers and markets, and finally to provide technical assistance in order to promote the establishment of national schemes.

48. The most important problem facing developing countries in financing their exports is perhaps the lack of financial resources. At the pre-shipment level, foreign exchange may not be available to import inputs needed for producing export goods. At the post-shipment level, foreign exchange constraint considerably weakens the ability of developing countries to extend credit on terms competitive with those offered by developed countries. In addition, as has been pointed out earlier, developed countries themselves are subsidizing their export credits. In order to compete with them effectively, besides the consideration of quality and price of the exported products, developing countries should have resources to subsidize their own export credits.

49. Proposals to address this problem are classified in two broad categories. The first category includes proposals to save foreign exchange payments, by way of a multilateral clearing arrangement.[8] Under such a clearing mechanism, intra-developing country trade can be settled without using foreign exchange, through the establishment of reciprocal external accounts to compensate imports and exports against each other. The need to hold liquid balances in foreign exchange deposited with banks in London, New York or other financial centres would be reduced. The costs to the traders of purchasing and selling foreign exchange could be eliminated. However, the effectiveness of these arrangements is limited, as the savings on transaction costs are small.

50. The second category of proposals aims at increasing the availability of foreign exchange resources and includes proposals for a regional or international financing and refinancing facility and proposals for guarantees of export credit paper. As

mentioned earlier, there exist for the present only three main regional mechanisms which effectively deal with the financing of export credit of developing countries: the Inter-American Development Bank refinancing mechanism, BLADEX financing mechanisms and the SAFICO financing mechanism, which are all located in the Latin American region. The Islamic Development Bank provides another potential mechanism. However, it should be noted that the size of these regional schemes is rather modest, as compared with the needs of member countries and that they are more concerned with intra-regional trade than trade among developing countries in general. In regions other than Latin America, a case can be made for the establishment of regional export financing or refinancing facilities, which might be associated with the regional development banks (such as the Asian and African Development Banks), to assist countries of these regions in financing their exports. Finally, an international facility can also be considered, which would provide finance to developing countries on a worldwide basis, especially if in some regions there is not enough cohesion between countries to form a regional scheme. An international facility might also have a better standing in international capital markets, enabling it to mobilize resources on more favourable terms.

51. Proposals for guarantees of export credit paper are also put forward to facilitate developing countries' access to international capital markets. A guarantee facility would require a smaller paid-in capital than a direct financing or refinancing scheme. By according its guarantee to export credit paper of developing countries, such a facility would improve the marketability of such paper in the international capital markets. The same reasons as those mentioned in the preceding paragraph in favour of the establishment of an international facility (versus regional) apply here.

52. Discussions on the establishment of an International Export Credit Guarantee Facility have taken place and detailed operational features of such a facility have been examined within UNCTAD. Because developing countries face difficulties mainly in the provision of medium- and long-term credit, the proposed Facility would cover the range of goods which are exported on such credit terms.

Notes

1. These are goods in the range of SITC (5 + 6 + 7 + 8) less SITC (67 + 68).
2. See the report by the UNCTAD secretariat entitled 'Institutional Arrangements in Developing Countries for Industrial and Export Finance with a view to Expanding and Diversifying their Exports of Manufactures and Semi-manufactures', United Nations Publication, Sales No. E.80.II.D.6, in particular Chapter II.
3. The OECD *Arrangement on Guidelines for Officially Supported Export Credits* has fixed minimum interest rates and maximum maturities on officially supported export credits to all recipient countries based on their per capita income. However, these minimum rates still remain low, as compared to lending rates by domestic banks of developed countries.
4. The IDB mechanism is functioning by rediscounting export credit portfolios of local central banks which have themselves discounted portfolios of their commercial banks. The financial sources are channelled through revolving lines of credit.
5. In an evaluation study on this mechanism, the IDB mentioned that the Venezuelan authorities have indicated their interest in reducing the use of the Venezuelan Trust Fund in export financing operations, in order to devote more resources to other long-term financing.
6. See, for example, the *Far Eastern Economic Review* of 15 February 1980.
7. Proposals for a regional export insurance scheme have aroused some interest in the Latin American, African and South East Asian regions.
8. Such a multilateral clearing arrangement has been under consideration in the context of regional trade financing of the eastern and southern African region and of the Asian region.

8 COMMODITY FINANCE

J. D. A. CUDDY

Introduction

1. The problems associated with the significant fluctuations in commodity prices both historically and particularly over the past decade are by now too well known to need rehearsing here. Nevertheless, despite the substantial attention devoted to these matters in various international forums, but particularly UNCTAD, during the past eight years only meagre results for commodity stabilization have been obtained. Since the adoption of the Integrated Programme for Commodities (IPC) in 1976, only one new international commodity agreement aimed at price stabilization has been concluded (rubber) whilst two others, which pre-dated the adoption of the IPC (tin and cocoa), have seen their effectiveness impaired and their very existence threatened. Indeed, at the time of writing (19 January 1982) even the rubber agreement's continued existence is in doubt. The sugar agreement, which also pre-dated the IPC, has been completely ineffectual in stabilizing the sugar market, and the coffee agreement (also pre-dating the IPC) has survived only thanks to the fortuitous frosts in Brazilian coffee-producing regions. Finally, the wheat agreement has been reduced to a shell with no operative economic provisions.

2. These events have been compounded by the failure even of high-level agreement at such meetings as Cancún to spur the process of ratification of the Common Fund for Commodities (which at present counts only nineteen of the necessary ninety ratifications). Moreover, the very structure of the Fund is such that it is not likely to provide much impetus to the conclusion of effective stabilization arrangements, since for operational purposes the Fund's stabilization window depends not only on the prior conclusion of such agreements, but also upon prior agreement of governments participating in such agreements

on the financing of at least one-third of the stocking requirements. Thus, any interest of commodity organizations in the use of the Fund will depend heavily on the Fund's marginal attractiveness *vis-à-vis* other sources of lending for all the remaining two-thirds of the financial requirements. This does not seem to add up to a new breakthrough in commodity stabilization finance.

An alternative approach

3. It would seem therefore that a fresh approach to the financing of commodity stabilization is necessary. The continued failure of producers and consumers to reach agreement on the terms of commodity stabilization, and the fact that the critical concern of developing commodity-exporting countries is to ensure that there is established a floor below which export prices would not be allowed to fall, and which would be sufficiently remunerative to producers that drastic reductions in employment in the commodity sector would not occur over a very short interval of time, lead to the conclusion that developing country producers ought to consider mechanisms by which they would ensure such a floor themselves.

4. It is, however, obvious that the financial circumstances of the developing producing countries would not allow the unilateral establishment of a global stocking scheme to support prices. Moreover, the alternative support mechanism, that of supply control, immediately confronts the difficulty of decision on the distribution of the short-term foreign exchange and employment sacrifices which are inherent in such measures. The history of attempts at producer co-operation in this regard is fraught with well-known failures on exactly this point.

5. These difficulties are particularly unfortunate in view of an important feature of stocking mechanisms to support commodity prices, which is that once they are perceived by the commodity markets to be credible, they are unlikely to need to have access to the financial resources which they apparently require. This result arises from the fact that commodity markets are highly liquid and attract substantial volumes of funds from both traders and speculators. If an operator in a commodity

market is convinced that the floor can be held, then, as the price nears this threshold, he will cover short positions and perhaps even go long on the commodity, thus supporting the floor price. If this is done in sufficient volume, the buffer stock may not need to expend much of its own resources in defending the floor.

6. Furthermore, since the financial resources of any buffer stock are finite, the ultimate line of defence of a floor price must be supply control. To the extent that the commodity markets perceive such control to be reliable and effective, the direct financial resources required by the buffer stock to defend the floor will be reduced. Thus, supply control measures can be an extremely important complement to a buffer stock, a principle recognized in the structure of the international tin agreement, which includes both these measures. Indeed, the existence of effective supply control measures should make a stocking scheme easily 'bankable' in the sense that it would attract private commercial finance since stock purchases are not consumption expenditure, but rather an investment in a durable asset which, given the observed cycles in commodity prices, should lead to significant capital gains as the stocks are sold into rising markets. This calculation can, of course, only be made if there is clear assurance that chronic production surpluses will not occur—hence the need for stand-by supply control measures if easy 'bankability' is to be achieved.

7. These considerations would seem to argue strongly for the establishment of a facility drawing upon commercial sources of finance, to support commodity prices via a combination of buffer stocks and stand-by supply control measures. Although it could be argued that the difficulties in reaching agreement on such supply control measures would be likely to vitiate such a scheme, it is arguable that the guarantee of sufficient funds to support an agreed floor price for a commodity, without the need to draw on the national treasury (except perhaps for some nominal participation in the form of contingent liabilities—i.e. callable capital), could transform even deep-seated recalcitrance into enthusiasm for such a scheme, thus assuring the very supply control necessary for the success of the scheme. It should be added that in most cases supply controls would be temporary rather than permanent.

8. By contrast with the Common Fund, such a scheme would focus on producers' activities only. Because geographical considerations make it unlikely that commodities of which industrialized countries are significant producers would be part of such a scheme, it would probably be limited initially to tropical agricultural products (the beverages, jute, hard fibres, tropical timber and rubber) and those minerals not produced in the 'North' (mainly tin, bauxite and cobalt). However, these commodities are of considerable importance to a large number of developing countries, among them many of the poorest. Moreover, the proposed scheme need not limit itself to the financing of internationally-held stocks, but could finance nationally-held stocks as well, so as to provide producing countries with the opportunity to withhold their supplies from the markets at times of depressed commodity prices, provided that adequate assurance would be obtained regarding the constitution of such stocks. Copper would be a major case, followed by some important vegetable oils.

Financing the proposed facility

9. The proposed facility should attract funding from commercial sources, including commercial banks, some of which might participate through interest-bearing loans to the facility, others of which might prefer to hold equity shares which would earn dividends based upon the capital gains made by the facility. A further vehicle for funding the facility might be the issue of 'commodity bonds', the holders of which would be entitled at maturity either to a fixed physical quantity of the commodity concerned, or to the revenue from the sale of a fixed quantity of the commodity. Depending upon the number of commodities financed by the facility, such revenue bonds might be issued on a multi-commodity basis, entailing fixed proportions of the various commodities; such bonds could be attractive to certain investors because of their risk-spreading nature.

9 THE FINANCING OF REGIONAL CREDIT ARRANGEMENTS AMONG DEVELOPING COUNTRIES

F. ABBATE

Introduction

1. It is widely recognized that, aside from simple clearing arrangements, a payments union endowed with resources for extending substantial medium-term balance of payments support to participants would be desirable to accelerate the expansion of trade among developing countries. Up to now, developing countries have established five multilateral credit arrangements among themselves. On the whole, forty-two developing countries participate in these arrangements (see Annexe 9.1). By providing balance of payments support in general, such arrangements promote at the same time broader economic integration and free-trade expansion objectives of the subregional groups formed by the participants. A common denominator of these schemes is the intention to supplement the balance of payments financing provided by the IMF. On the whole, the existing five agreements contemplate balance of payments credits which amount to approximately US $1.6 billion. This is a very modest amount when compared to the aggregate reserves of the forty-two participating countries and to their balance of payments needs.

Existing proposals

2. A financial linkage among the five regional schemes has been recommended for quite some time, especially by the Co-ordination Committee on multilateral payments arrangements and monetary co-operation. One way to achieve it would be through the establishment among these arrangements of a surplus liquidity reserve pool. In such a system, different groups of developing countries would be supporting each other,

instead of depositing their surplus funds with private international banks in good times and borrowing from them in bad times. In a reciprocal arrangement of this type, since banking intermediation is bypassed, the cost of borrowing might be lowered, without affecting the rate of return to the lender. At present, however, this scheme would apply only to those arrangements which actually hold foreign exchange resources, i.e. the Arab Monetary Fund, the Andean Reserve Fund and the Central American Monetary Stabilization Fund. The other two arrangements operate on reciprocal lines of credit among participating central banks.

3. The pooling of foreign exchange reserves among regional credit arrangements would certainly bring about an increase in the loanable funds available to each individual scheme, relying on the reasonable assumption that not all institutions will need to draw on reserves at the same time.

A new proposal

4. The financial benefits deriving from pooling, however, may be dwarfed by the large balance of payments needs of some member countries. Thus, in addition to the foreign exchange reserves of the participants themselves, there is a need for external resources, in order to enlarge the volume of funds available to each arrangement. The merging of participants' own resources and external capital could be effected within a new institution, a Common Stabilization Fund.

5. A Common Stabilization Fund (CSF) could function in the following manner:

(a) each participating institution deposits a certain percentage of its reserve assets, say 25 per cent, with the CSF. Credit lines with central banks could be temporarily accepted, as a proxy for foreign exchange reserves, from those arrangements which do not rely on reserve pooling. Deposits are remunerated at near-market rates;
(b) each participating institution retains an automatic right to its deposits, and under certain conditions may draw from a line of credit which is twice the amount of the deposit;

(c) conditionality attached to CSF loans is related mainly to an assessment of regional economic co-operation and monitoring of their implementation;
(d) loans extended by the CSF are jointly guaranteed by the member countries of the borrowing participating institution. Such loans carry near-market interest rates;
(e) the CSF is empowered to borrow from public and private sources up to 200 per cent of its deposits;
(f) the CSF would probably need a small interest-free capital base which could be used to meet short-term liquidity needs, and to subsidize market borrowing.

The interest of surplus developing countries

6. Capital-surplus developing countries may find it attractive to become lenders to the CSF. In the example above, if the initial pooling is limited to 25 per cent of reserves, deposits of potential participating institutions—the existing five credit arrangements—would amount to some $400 million. The corresponding maximum borrowing requirements of the CSF would be $800 million. Lending by the surplus developing countries to the CSF could be along the same lines as the recent loans by the Saudi Arabia Monetary Agency to the IMF. The availability of a balance of payments facility associated with regional co-operation schemes should act as a powerful catalyst for new initiatives in the field of financial co-operation among developing countries, such as the creation of additional and more ambitious regional credit arrangements.

7. The establishment of a limited CSF would be a first step towards evolving a broader mutual payments arrangements within the developing world in which the surplus oil-exporting countries are assured of an effective voice so that they can confidently entrust it with a part of their surpluses.

8. In formulating this type of arrangement the whole-hearted participation of the oil-exporting countries is as necessary as the willingness on the part of the non-oil developing countries to assure them that their surpluses will enjoy the same standards of liquidity, profitability and safety, as with the private banking system.

Conclusions

9. It is realized that the proposal put forward in this note needs to be further elaborated, to take into account, *inter alia*, the actual interest for such a proposal on the part of existing arrangements and possible lenders. Admittedly, the kind of monetary co-operation implied by the CSF would be the result of a long-term process which is amenable to a step-by-step approach. The first step could be the extension of credit lines and swaps between regional schemes.

10. The Common Stabilization Fund could be a separate entity, linked with the other ECDC financial mechanisms, such as the one on joint ventures (see document 2 in this series) and others in the suggested South Bank Group; or it could be one lending window of the proposed South Bank.

Annex 9.1 Regional credit arrangements among developing countries

Entity		Participating countries countries	Resources (US $ million)
1. Arab Monetary Fund	(20)	Algeria, Bahrain, Egypt, Iraq, Jordan, Kuwait, Lebanon, Libyan Arab Jamahiriya, Mauritania, Morocco, Oman, People's Democratic Republic of Yemen, Qatar, Saudi Arabia, Somalia, Sudan, Syrian Arab Republic, Tunisia, United Arab Emirates and Yemen Arab Republic	945
2. Andean Reserve Fund	(5)	Bolivia, Colombia, Ecuador, Peru and Venezuela	240
3. ASEAN Swap Arrangement	(5)	Indonesia, Malaysia, Philippines, Singapore and Thailand	200
4. Central American Monetary Stabilization Fund	(5)	Costa Rica, El Salvador, Guatemala, Honduras and Nicaragua	63

Annexe 9.1 (*cont.*)

Entity	Participating countries		Resources (US $ million)
5. Latin American Free Trade Association's Financial Assistance Agreement	(12)	Argentina, Bolivia, Brazil, Colombia, Chile, Dominican Republic, Ecuador, Mexico, Paraguay, Peru, Uruguay and Venezuela	263
Total	42[1]		1,631

[1] Countries participating in more than one scheme have been counted only once.

10 PAYMENTS ARRANGEMENTS FOR OIL IMPORTS

F. ABBATE

Introduction

1. Oil imports are only one item of the balance of payments of developing countries. In many of them, particularly the poorer, they are lower in magnitude than imports of foodstuffs. None the less, they represent a very heavy element; and as most oil is imported from other developing countries, it is natural that, in ECDC efforts, attention is turned to the possibility of alleviating balance of payments pressures on oil-importing developing countries (OIDCs) through promotion of energy investment and through special payments arrangements for oil imports.

2. More broadly, an integrated international strategy aiming at alleviating the energy problems faced by OIDCs should encompass the following key elements:

(a) the guarantee to ensure a minimum level of oil supplies during periods of acute scarcity;
(b) the provision of financial assistance for oil imports, particularly at the time of sharp rises in oil prices;
(c) the mobilization of medium- and long-term financing for development of their energy resources.

This note lists a number of policy options for implementing the measure mentioned under (b) above. The issues involved in financing energy investment were discussed in another note.

Financing the oil deficit

3. Apart from the two-tier oil price system which could generate major distortions in oil trading, there are several other ways in which surplus developing countries may assist OICDs in meeting the increased cost of oil imports:

(i) the creation of a special facility for this purpose in existing international financial institutions along the lines of the temporary Oil Facility which the IMF operated in 1974–5. Access to that facility, however, was subject to the conditionality rules of the IMF;

(ii) the establishment of an independent multilateral facility, providing concessional loans and grants for oil purchases by developing countries, with no conditionality attached to drawings. The amount of financing could be linked either to a certain percentage of oil imports or, as in the case of the IMF's compensatory financing of fluctuations in the cost of cereal imports, to excesses in the cost of oil imports caused by factors beyond their control, such as a temporary decline in domestic oil production or a sharp increase in oil import prices;

(iii) the provision of medium- or long-term loans repayable in foreign exchange at market-related floating rates of interest for a part of oil imports, with no conditionality attached to drawings;

(iv) the provision of bilateral assistance, as in the case of a number of OAPEC countries and Nigeria, or subregional financial assistance along the lines of Trinidad and Tobago's action in favour of the Caribbean subregion and the recent Mexican–Venezuelan initiative. The latter entails the assured supply by Mexico and Venezuela of one-half of the oil needs of a number of Caribbean and Central American countries, and 30 per cent of the value of this supply is financed by five-year loans carrying an interest rate of 4 per cent. However, if the loans are used for capital investment projects in the economy, especially for the development of indigenous energy resources, the loan terms become an interest rate of 2 per cent with a twenty-year repayment period;

(v) the acceptance of payment in local currency for part of oil imports by OIDCs. Local currency proceeds could be used by surplus countries for different purposes, including the financing of local currency expenditures incurred in connection with the development of joint ventures with OIDCs (see Chapter 4 of this book).

4. It should be further recalled that the report of the OPEC

Ministerial Committee on Long-Term Strategy suggested that OPEC might assist OIDCs with regard to the payment of the increase in the cost of their oil imports. The report proposed that for this purpose OIDCs might be grouped into three categories according to their per capita income and size of their oil imports:

— less developed countries with a per capita income below $300 whose oil imports are in the range of 10,000 b/d each would be given grants or interest-free, long-term loans;
— countries whose per capita income is between $300 and $1,000 and oil imports between 10,000 and 100,000 b/d would be given concessional long-term loans, with a 25–50 per cent grant element;
— countries whose per capita income is more than $1,000 or imports more than 100,000 b/d would be given medium-term loans on a commercial basis.

The report stressed that although the financing of an increased cost of $2 per barrel of oil imports by OIDCs would have totalled $3.3 billion in 1980, commercial loans would have represented the lion's share, with grants and grant element of concessional loans only amounting to some $360–700 million. This is due to the fact that the relatively richer OIDCs account for the bulk of total oil imports by OIDCs.

5. In considering these possibilities, an important point to bear in mind is that a number of oil-exporting countries are at present experiencing current account deficits due, to a considerable extent, to the the weakness of the international oil market. Hence their ability to provide special terms for oil exports is constrained. Even some of the countries in a strong balance of payments position have seen their oil revenues decline very sharply during the last year. If special terms for oil payments are introduced, due care will have to be taken to assure an appropriate sharing of the burden and allocation of benefits to those who need assistance most.

11 PROMOTION OF INVESTMENT FLOWS AMONG DEVELOPING COUNTRIES: SOUTH–SOUTH MULTILATERAL INVESTMENT GUARANTEE SCHEMES

VIJAY L. KELKAR

I

1. Collective self-reliance is one of the key components of the strategy for the establishment of the NIEO. Equally, the concept of collective self-reliance is now recognized to be central to the efforts of the developing countries in promoting economic co-operation among themselves. At the very least collective self-reliance signifies two important dimensions: (i) strengthening of intra-developing countries' linkages so as to accelerate the growth of productive forces of the developing countries, and (ii) promotion of an autonomous development process in the national economies of developing countries by minimizing their dependence on the developed countries. In other words, it seeks to inject more 'symmetry' as well as dynamism to the world economy. It should be noted that perhaps the most important aspect of collective self-reliance is the promotion of mutually beneficial economic relations which are truly symmetric.

2. To achieve this, it is clear that bold initiatives will have to be taken in the field of trade, i.e. trade expansion among developing countries; in the field of finance, i.e. promotion of investment flows both concessional and commercial; in the field of technology, i.e. technical collaboration, flows of human capital, co-operation in research and development, etc. It is suggested that in the formulation of an appropriate policy package that would ensure success in the above areas, the promotion of financial flows and investment flows among developing countries is of strategic importance. In this regard the post-war experience of the industrialized countries of rapid economic

expansion is quite instructive. In the recent Trade and Development Report of UNCTAD, the post-war period is described as a period which promoted 'collective self-reliance' among industrialized countries.[1] It should be noted that during this period, movement of financial flows from capital surplus countries to deficit countries among the industrialized world played a key role in sustaining economic growth, technological progress and trade expansion. In some ways, these flows were of even greater importance in promoting economic linkages than commercial policy measures taken by these countries.[2] Given the present international economic environment as well as the needs of various groups of developing countries, acceleration of financial flows amongst developing countries has now become of even greater importance and urgency.

3. Such measures of financial co-operation are of critical importance to both capital-surplus developing countries as well as to capital-deficit developing countries. It should be noted that the capital-surplus countries, i.e. OPEC countries, have taken various important measures for channelling concessional financial flows to other developing countries. In fact, as a percentage of gross national product, such transfers from OPEC countries to other developing countries far exceed the performance of the OECD economies.[3] These resource flows have been handled by a very well-developed national and multilateral institutional framework created by the OPEC countries.[4] There is no doubt that these institutions will have to continue their efforts of promoting concessional flows to other developing countries. However, it is clear that, at the margin, the growth rates of investment flows will be much greater in the area of non-concessional flows, i.e. commercial flows from OPEC countries to other developing countries. This point has been made by many a spokesman of the OPEC countries. This development is due to many well-known reasons whose strength has to be appreciated. It is suggested that the institutional framework, however, is not yet sufficiently well developed to help accelerate such flows among developing countries. Such an institutional framework is also of value to developing countries other than OPEC countries as there are increasing possibilities of promoting intra-developing countries' investment flows originating from non-OPEC developing countries.

4. It has to be recognized that greater investment flows from capital-surplus countries to other developing countries would promote mutual interests. There is increasing feeling in OPEC countries that they are 'over-exposed' in OECD countries in terms of their holdings of short-term and long-term assets in those markets. The inherent risks of such a situation were dramatically revealed when the USA took action against Iran's assets in that country in 1980. As observed by Dr. Nuwayhid, one of the most perceptive analysts, diversification of investments should be a key component of the strategy of the capital-surplus countries to ensure their investments.[5] As noted by Dr. Nuwayhid, OAPEC, a sub-set of OPEC countries, will continue to record substantial surpluses during the next decade and will have to diversify their assets as a part of long-term strategy. According to his study, by 1980 out of US $270 billion of OAPEC foreign assets almost 90 per cent were deployed in the form of financial assets and almost all of it was in OECD countries. He has suggested that over the next ten to fifteen years the investment mix should be such that out of total assets only 40 per cent will be financial assets and out of the 'real assets', i.e. 60 per cent of the total assets, 70 per cent should be in Third World countries, including other Arab countries. In the light of the present mix, this may be an ambitious target given the existent institutional framework as well as absorptive capacity of the developing countries.

However, it can be argued that to achieve this kind of qualitative change in investments, whether from public sector investors or private investors of capital-exporting countries, they would like to be assured of (i) commercial profitability of their investments and (ii) political security about the protection of their investments. Such guarantees that would promote investments are, of course, also important from the viewpoint of the capital-importing countries not only because of the obvious importance of acceleration of investments in their economies but also because of their likely favourable impact on the international oil market. It has to be recognized that increasingly the international financial markets or international capital markets and world oil markets are becoming inter-dependent because of the fact that oil is an exhaustible or non-renewable resource, and consequently its rate of depletion would crucially depend upon the strength and security of investments of capital-surplus

OPEC countries. Hence, diversification in allocation of investment flows would help the capital-surplus economies in improving the expected yields on their foreign investments. Such an improvement can have only a favourable impact on oil supplies from the viewpoint of OPEC. Perhaps the most important argument could be that such investment flows to other developing countries would only strengthen the OPEC in terms of their bargaining with the OECD countries.

5. Although it is true that in the initial years inter-governmental investment projects would play a leading role in promoting investments amongst developing countries, over time this would undergo a change. Providing guarantees against non-commercial or political risks may be of growing importance in increasing investment flows, as it is expected that private investors and financial institutions will play an important role in deployment of private savings of the capital-surplus, oil-exporting countries, This trend is already evident by the fact that a number of private financial institutions are emerging in the capital-surplus, oil-exporting countries. Equally, there is a new and growing trend of industrial joint ventures promoted by developing countries in other developing countries by either public sector or the private sector enterprises of the developing countries themselves.[6] There are a number of developing countries which now possess capabilities of technology transfer to other developing countries, and such mutually beneficial technology transfer can be encouraged if one can minimize the political or non-commercial risks. It should be noted that developed countries have created multilateral and national instruments which provide such insurance or guarantees to the private investors and these schemes have played an important role. It is suggested here that the developing countries may consider creating an appropriate South–South multilateral framework that would insure investors against non-commercial risks in their investments.

6. It must be recognized that amongst the developing countries there is no overall consensus yet on the issue of providing such a guarantee or insurance, in principle. It is sometimes pointed out that past attempts to reach agreement on investment guarantees have failed; they would discriminate against domestic

investors; and they would impose an unwarranted financial cost (through payment of insurance premiums) on countries which have not engaged and do not engage in political and other acts adverse to foreign investment. It is further suggested that as it is the governments in the capital-importing countries which are anxious to attract capital, they would not engage in expropriation and similar acts and therefore the issue of guarantees does not arise. All these different considerations must be discussed further. In what follows a possible scheme is worked out to facilitate such a discussion.

II

7. The existence of an institutional framework is widely recognized as being of critical importance in promoting international investments. Amongst other things, an institutional framework would include depth and width of national capital markets, legal framework, e.g. assurance of non-discrimination, etc., information flows about investment projects and markets, dispute settlements and arbitration procedures, and insurance guarantee schemes.[7] The importance of a multilateral treaty for protection of investments was recognized even in the Havana Charter in 1948, and in fact it finds a place in the Articles of the draft Charter. Other similar efforts were undertaken, such as the Bogota Agreement of 1948. However, these efforts did not succeed in creating legal instruments.[8] Similarly, there have been considerable efforts at different forums such as IBRD and OECD which attempted to draw multilateral investment guarantee schemes involving both industrialized and developing countries. These efforts have not succeeded as a result of differences amongst industrialized countries, and more importantly because of political problems which arose among the developing countries, especially those of Latin America. The countries of Latin America have argued that such multilateral arbitration, which is implied in investment guarantee schemes, goes against the 'Calvo Doctrine'; namely, it discriminates in favour of foreign investors compared to national investors by giving the possibilities to foreign investors of going outside their domestic laws and procedures. One should be aware that perhaps behind these legal arguments the political issues have involved political problems bearing on the

relationship of the major investing countries in that region and individual Latin American countries. It is, of course, not clear whether the objections of Latin American countries would continue to multilateral investment guarantee schemes where participation is voluntary and restricted only to the developing countries, i.e. South–South investment guarantee scheme. In such a situation, it can be argued that the underlying political aspects are of an entirely different nature and the legitimate fear which countries of Latin America have regarding the powerful developed countries need not exist *vis-à-vis* other developing countries.[9] Against this argument is the point that it would be somewhat difficult to give guarantees to one group of investors—from developing countries—and not to the other group—from developed countries.

8. The OECD countries have taken numerous measures—national, bilateral and multilateral—for the encouragement of investment flows. For instance, the Tready of Rome defines rights and obligations of foreign investors. In fact, in the EEC, in addition to national laws, there are community laws as well as the European Convention for Protection of Foreign Investment.[10] OECD has adopted a Convention on the protection of foreign property which contains various articles regarding fair and equitable treatment, security of foreign investments, ensuring non-discrimination against foreign investors, procedures for dispute settlement, etc.[11] It must be noted that even this Convention *does not* deny the countries the right to nationalize or to control investments according to their national policies. In addition to this Convention, there are other instruments developed by OECD for facilitating capital movements and for improving the functioning of capital markets. For instance, OECD has adopted a Code of Liberalization of Capital Movements. It is clear that the developing countries have not yet reached a stage where they can fully liberalize capital movements among themselves and this process may have to wait for a considerable amount of time to come.

9. As far as OECD investments in developing countries are concerned, these are now governed by bilateral agreements between developed countries and various individual developing countries.[12] These bilateral agreements do incorporate

understanding regarding the principles of non-discrimination, equitable and fair treatment, dispute settlements, etc. Given these bilateral agreements, individual states of OECD formulated their national schemes for investment guaranteees which provide insurance against political or non-commercial risks. The oldest is that of the USA which by 1976 had a total liability for investment insurance exceeding $10 billion. Equally, the national scheme of Germany is quite vigorous and by 1975 it had made commitments to investments of 2.5 billion DM.[13]

10. The existence and growth of these schemes shows the importance of an institutional mechanism that provides insurance against political risk. As far as developing countries are concerned, it seems that a multilateral framework is of much greater relevance compared to the bilateral framework that exists in the OECD countries. This is due to various reasons: a multilateral framework would be more equitable, more cost-efficient and less politicized. Such a framework would be more efficient as, given the large number of developing countries, bilateral agreements would be too many, would take much longer time and could lead to higher transaction costs. In addition, there is now a growing tendency towards 'multinational' projects, i.e. projects involving more than two countries where purely bilateral agreements or frameworks would not be adequate in promoting such projects. Finally, a multilateral agreement or framework would create far fewer legal or constitutional problems for many of the developing countries. All this points to the desirability of having a multilateral framework for insurance and a guarantee of foreign investments among developing countries. Our proposed scheme is based on the study of existing national insurance schemes as well as multilateral schemes.

11. At the outset it should be noted that participation in the suggested scheme would be voluntary and open only to the developing countries.

12. It is clear that the proposed multilateral investment guarantee corporation may have to be part of a multilateral convention which would spell out the legal framework, such as the principle of fair and equitable treatment, non-discrimination,

principle of compensation, principle and procedures of dispute settlement, etc., and the proposed investment guarantee cooperation would be open only to the signatories of this convention. It is suggested that initially the period of enforcement of such a convention could be for twenty years. Such a time limit may encourage greater participation.

13. In designing a multilateral scheme it should be noted that there are two distinct models that are available: one as indicated by the IBRD in its draft on international investment insurance agency, and the other one is that of the Inter-Arab Investment Guarantee Corporation created by eighteen Arab States and which has been in existence since 1972.[14] It should be noted that the first one is a North–South institution, while the other one is purely a South institution. With regard to the types of investment covered, eligibility criteria, etc., there is a great deal of similarity in these two models. However, there are very important and qualitative differences. In the IBRD model the losses are shared only by capital-exporting countries and consequently the voting strength is not equitable; for example, capital-exporting industrialized countries have two-thirds and capital-importing countries have one-third of the votes. By comparison, in the Inter-Arab Guarantee Corporation the risk is shared by all shareholders; that is, there is no distinction between capital-surplus and capital-deficit countries and the voting pattern is much more democratic. Of course, for the participating countries, their contribution of equity capital defines the limit of their total liability. In working out our proposal, we have chosen the model of the Inter-Arab Investment Guarantee Corporation as it is more equitable, given the objective of collective self-reliance, as well as more logical, given the fact that amongst developing countries there is no precise distinction of capital-importing or capital-exporting countries that can be maintained which is valid for every investment or every region.

Risk coverage

14. The proposed corporation would cover three types of noncommercial or political risks: (i) expropriation risks, (ii) transfer risks and (iii) war risks, as described below:

(a) Measures taken by the public authorities in the host country, either directly or through an agency, whereby the investor is deprived of his substantial rights with respect to his investment and, in particular, confiscatory measures, nationalization, sequestration, expropriation, compulsory seizure, deprivation of a creditor of his rights including the right of assignment, and the imposition of moratoriums of unreasonable length.

(b) Introduction by the public authorities in the host country, either directly or through an agency, of new measures which substantially restrict the ability of the investor to repatriate the principal of his investment or to remit his earnings therefrom or the investment amortization instalments. The above position shall be constructed to include a delay for an unreasonable period in approving the transfer, as well as the imposition by the public authorities at the time of transfer of a rate of exchange which is clearly discriminatory against the investor.

The risk provided for in this paragraph shall not be deemed to include measures existing at the time of conclusion of the insurance contract and shall not include general devaluation of currency or cases of exchange depreciation.

(c) Any military action emanating from a foreign source or from the host country which directly affects the tangible assets of the investor, and all public civil disturbances such as revolutions, *coups d'état*, insurrections and acts of violence of a public character having the same effect.

15. Insurance contracts shall state specifically the risks covered by the insurance in each case. In all cases the insurance contract shall not cover losses arising from any measures taken by the public authorities in the host country in any of the following cases:

(a) where such measures can be provided against by ordinary insurance transactions on reasonable terms;

(b) where the investor has expressly agreed to such measures being taken or has been directly responsible for them;

(c) where the measures are such as a state may normally take for the purpose of regulating economic activity in its territory and which do not involve discrimination against the investor by the insurance.

16. The corporation shall in no case assume responsibility for commercial risks that attend the insured investment.

Eligibility criteria

17. It is proposed that only new investments will be eligible and these investments could be in the form of equity, portfolio or contribution of technology, e.g. patent or industrial property rights or technology transfer in the form of long-term service contracts. Investment eligible for the coverage will have to be approved by the host government. The eligible investments are detailed below.

(1) Investments eligible for insurance shall comprise all investments between the contracting countries whether they are direct investments (including enterprises and their branches or agencies, ownership of a part of capital and ownership of real estate), or portfolio investments (including ownership of share, stocks and bonds), or in the sharing of technology or industrial property rights. Eligible investments also comprise loans for a term exceeding three years as well as such shorter term loans as the governing council may in exceptional cases decide to treat as eligible for insurance.
(2) In identifying investments for the purpose of preceding paragraph, the corporation shall be assisted by the guidelines issued by the International Monetary Fund on the definition of long-term assets and liabilities in the context of the preparation of balance of payments statistics.
(3) In appraising the eligibility of an investment for the purpose of insurance, no distinction shall be made on account of the monetary or non-monetary form of the transaction. Reinvestment of earnings accrued out of a previous investment shall also be eligible for insurance.
(4) Insurance shall not be available except for new investments which are made after the conclusion of an insurance contract.
(5) Private investments and other mixed and public investments operating on a commercial basis shall be eligible for insurance.
(6) The conclusion of insurance contracts shall be subject to

the condition that the investor shall have obtained the prior approval of the competent official authority in the host country for the making of the investment and for its insurance with the corporation against the risks to be covered.

18. As far as insurance limit is concerned, it could be for the entire amount of the investment or part of the amount. The proposed corporation will be a separate legal entity. It is suggested that a dispute settlement mechanism will need to be spelled out—this could be either on the lines of the Hague Convention on Arbitration or the International Centre for Settlement of Investment Disputes (ICSID) in Washington. The latter Convention has been signed by more than sixty countries including many developing countries. Any such procedures would stipulate the rules for conciliation and arbitration.

Financial structure and premiums

19. Taking into account the long-term objectives of capital-surplus countries as well as the potential of industrial joint ventures, it is suggested that over the period of the next five years or so this corporation may have to handle or insure investment of the order of US $5 billion. The equity capital basis of the corporation which can support such liabilities would depend upon the experience that would be built up by the corporation. For instance, in the USA for their investment guarantee operation the ratio of total liability to equity exceeds 10. The Inter-Arab Investment Guarantee Corporation works with much lower ratios, i.e. 1:5. In the initial stages it is suggested that the proposed corporation may have to work with a lower ratio, somewhere between 5 and 10. This would suggest that such an equity base of this corporation would have to exceed $500 million. Naturally, such a capital base would be subscribed in phases and contributions towards this would be made by every signatory. The exact amount of contribution would consist of an equal predetermined amount for each of the countries plus the voluntary contribution. In the initial stage perhaps the corporation could be launched with an equity base of, say $100 million with every participating country contributing an equity of $1 million and the remaining

amount being shared on a voluntary basis.[15] Premium charges of the corporation would ultimately depend on the cost structure. As far as international experience is concerned, the premium rates vary from 0.8 to 1.5 per cent. It is possible that the corporation, as in US practice, could charge 0.5 per cent for every three risks that are covered, i.e. 1.5 per cent in total where all three types of the risks are to be covered.

Management structure

20. It is understood that only developing countries would be eligible for the membership of this proposed convention and hence for the shareholdership of the proposed multilateral investment guarantee investment corporation. As far as management structure is concerned, it is suggested that we follow the current practice that exists in other similar inter-governmental institutions; namely, having a governing body where every government that is a signatory or a shareholder is a member and which lays down the broad policy of the corporation while the policy implementation is supervised by a Board of Executive Directors appointed by the Governing Council. Such a Board of Executive Directors would be presided over by a managing director who would be the chief executive of the corporation. The voting strength of individual member countries would depend upon their own contribution to the equity capital. Needless to say, there are various other details which would require further elaboration. Admittedly at this stage we have given only an illustrative outline of the proposed agency or corporation.

21. Before we conclude, it has to be noted that in addition to these investment guarantees there are various other promotional measures that can be undertaken under the proposed convention to promote investment flows amongst developing countries. These promotional measures would include, among other things, fiscal incentives, harmonization of tax laws, etc. Other measures may be also organized which would promote commercial attractiveness of these investments. These measures relate to the market information, greater dissemination about investment opportunities, greater exchange of information regarding national investment programmes and plans, etc.

Notes

1. UNCTAD *Trade and Development Report*, Geneva, 1981, p. 28.
2. See Vijay Kelkar, *Reflections on Post-War Growth in World Trade in Manufactures*, Geneva, 1981 (mimeo). Available from author on request.
3. For a recent analysis see UNCTAD *Financial Solidarity for Development*, Geneva, 1979 (TD/B/C.7/31).
4. For details see J. W. Salacuse, 'Arab Capital and Middle Eastern Development Finance—The Existing International Framework', *Journal of World Trade Law*, 1980.
5. H. Nuwayhid, 'Investment and Protection of OAPEC Surpluses', *Organization of Arab Petroleum Exporting Countries Bulletin*, February 1981.
6. There is a growing literature on industrial joint ventures amongst developing countries. For details see UNIDO *Structural Changes in Industry*, Vienna, 1981, pp. 41-52.
7. The importance of these aspects was brought out as early as the 1960s by the UN. See UN, *Foreign Investment in Developing Countries*, New York, 1968.
8. For details see R. Gardener, 'Institutional Measures for Promotion and Protection of Foreign Investment', *Journal of Public Law*, 1960.
9. Even in a strictly legal sense it has been argued that the multilateral investment guarantees need not be irreconcilable with the Calvo clause, as *distinctions without discrimination* are available in the national investment laws of numerous countries of Latin America. However, here there are complex issues involved and we are not taking a position one way or the other.
10. For details see W. H. Balekjian, *Legal Aspects of Foreign Investments in the EEC*, Manchester University Press, 1967.
11. OECD, *Draft Convention on the Protection of Foreign Property*, Paris, 1968.
12. It is interesting to note that such bilateral agreements exist between a few Latin American countries and some OECD countries.
13. For a discussion of these national schemes see OECD *The Experience of OECD in Promoting Investment Among OECD Countries and Between Them and Developing Countries*, Paris, 1978.
14. See (i) IBRD, Draft Articles of Agreement of International Investment Insurance Agency, Washington D.C., USA, 19 February 1972, and (ii) Inter-Arab Investment Guarantee Corporation, The Convention, Kuwait, 1978.
15. It may be noted here that the capital base of the US organization exceeds $400 million and the equity capital base of the Inter-Arab Investment Guarantee Corporation is $50 million.

12 CONCESSIONAL DEVELOPMENT ASSISTANCE BY OPEC MEMBERS AND INSTITUTIONS TO OTHER DEVELOPING COUNTRIES

HASSAN QAQAYA

Introduction

1. Within the general theme of financial co-operation among developing countries the present chapter focuses on development finance provided by nine members of OPEC to other developing countries on concessional terms over the period 1977–80. Both bilateral flows and flows channelled through multilateral agencies are covered. The data are complete when the assistance is provided through national and international financial institutions whose reports have been used. These data have been supplemented by data on government-to-government flows as reported to UNCTAD by the respective governments, in the case of Qatar, the United Arab Emirates, Iraq and Venezuela. With respect to assistance provided by Algeria, Iran, Libya and Saudi Arabia, primary data have not been adequately reported, and therefore it has been necessary to resort to secondary sources to complement the information.

2. In this chapter, development assistance refers to long-term finance provided on concessionary terms. In compliance with conventional usage by the Development Assistance Committee (DAC), concessionality has been defined as applying to loans with a grant element of at least 25 per cent, based on a discount rate of 10 per cent.

3. For purposes of this chapter, developing countries refer to those countries appearing on the standard list used by UNCTAD for recipients of development assistance (i.e. developing countries in Asia, Africa and Latin America).

4. This chapter contains general review of the magnitudes and

trends and the distinguishing features of OPEC assistance, providing the aggregate picture and then the assessment of activities of multilateral and national OPEC aid institutions as a group. (A country-by-country and institution-by-institution review of individual OPEC donors and institutions may be obtained from the author on request.)

5. The ECDC Staff Group wishes to acknowledge the assistance and advice provided by the governments and staff of the OPEC countries concerned and their financial institutions, as well as of the OECD–DAC staff, Paris.

The overall view

6. One of the most important new sources of finance available to developing countries since the mid-1970s has been the flow from OPEC countries as they greatly expanded the scope and scale of their aid activities. Most OPEC members have set up their own national agencies and helped to create multilateral institutions for channelling financial assistance to other developing countries. There are now four active national institutions: the Kuwait Fund for Arab Economic Development, the Iraq Fund for External Development, the Abu Dhabi Fund for Arab Economic Development and the Saudi Fund for Development. At the international level, in addition to their contributions to the capital of the World Bank, the facilities of the IMF, and transfers to IDA, OPEC members have been instrumental in creating multilateral institutions which are financed by them either in total or in large measure. The OPEC Fund for International Development (OFID) is exclusively financed by OPEC members. The Arab Fund for Economic and Social Development (AFESD), the Islamic Development Bank (ISDB) and the Banque Arabe pour le Développement en Afrique (BADEA) are financed by OPEC members. Moreover, there are national institutions which are concerned with concessional assistance and also engage in commercial activities in developing countries. This refers in particular to recent activities of the Venezuelan Investment Fund and the Libyan Foreign Trade Bank.

7. In recent years, the performance of OPEC members as a group has been adversely affected by the developments in Iran

and the war in the Gulf. Nevertheless, total concessional commitments to developing countries by nine members of OPEC increased by 76 per cent between 1977 and 1980 from US $7,335 million to US $12,920 million, an amount which represents a level of assistance approximately four times higher than that of seven years earlier (1973). Total cumulative commitments during the period 1977–80 amounted to US $40,325.3 million.

8. While the overall total commitments for nine members of OPEC followed a general upward trend, with the exception of a setback in 1978, the experiences of individual donor countries differed. Thus, while Qatar and Iraq continued to increase their commitments from US $104.5 million and US $218.5 million in 1977 to US $616.8 million and US $2,202 million in 1980 respectively, Algeria's and Libya's commitments declined in 1979 before increasing again in 1980. In terms of absolute flows, Saudi Arabia accounted for US $11,970 million, or almost 29.6 per cent of total cumulative commitments, followed by Kuwait (US $8,986.7 million or 22.3 per cent), Venezuela (US $6,877 million or 17.6 per cent), United Arab Emirates (US $4,405.7 million or 10.9 per cent), Iraq (US $4,206.7 million or 10.4 per cent), Libya (US $1,764 million or about 4.3 per cent), Qatar (US $1,288.8 million or almost 3.2 per cent), and Algeria (US $825.6 million or about 2.0 per cent) (see Table 1).

9. Total disbursements for the period under review followed roughly a similar trend as that of commitments. The difference is due to the time-lag between commitments, which are often concentrated in one given year, and disbursements, which may be spread over several years, particularly in the case of project-oriented loans. On the whole, however, the disbursements have moved quite rapidly. Since at the end of the period there was an outstanding undisbursed balance of US $7,645 million, it is possible that the level of disbursements may remain at a relatively high level in 1981 and subsequently even if commitments were to suffer a decline, but not for too long.

10. The proportion of national income devoted to assistance has differed from country to country. The average has been

Table 1 Concessional financial flows to developing countries, bilateral and multilateral[a] (US $ million)

	Commitments				Disbursements			
	1977	1978	1979	1980	1977	1978	1979	1980
Algeria[d]	171.5	228.8	163.3	262.0[b]	102.1	228.8	163.3	262.0
Iran	290.2	12.0	0.1	57.7[c]	211.0	278.0	25.0	3.0
Iraq	218.6	603.3	1,182.8	2,504.9[b]	111.8	563.8	1,028.8	2,202.8
Libyan Arab Jamahiriya	222.6	605.1	211.6	725.3	121.2	524.1	429.6	217.9
Kuwait	1,851.2	1,793.9	1,988.9	3,352.7	1,433.3	1,685.6	1,847.4	1,482.8
Qatar	104.5	214.2	353.3	616.8	102.7	214.5	249.8	591.3
Saudi Arabia	2,512.1	2,128.3	3,412.6	3,917.8	2,303.8	1,981.0	2,901.3	3,230.5
United Arab Emirates	1,214.1	875.2	1,097.6	1,218.8	1,577.2	779.6	1,117.6	1,210.6
Venezuela	1,041.0	528.0	673.0	625.0	723.0	746.0	494.0	612.0
Total	7,625.8	6,988.8	9,083.2	13,281.0	6,686.1	7,001.4	8,256.8	9,812.9

[a] Includes contributions to IDA.
[b] Both Algeria and Iraq report only disbursed pledges. Commitments may exceed the figures reported here.
[c] Source: DAC Chairman Report, 1981.
[d] These figures are based on preliminary estimates by the Algerian Ministry of Finance.

Source: Financial Solidarity for Development, Efforts and Institutions of the Members of OPEC 1977-1981 Review, UNCTAD Publication TD/B/893 (forthcoming).

going down in the three years 1978–80, but only in 1980 both the mean and the median declined, the former from 2.99 per cent in 1979 to 2.72 per cent in 1980, and the latter from 3.38 per cent to 3.15 per cent (Table 2). None the less, the performance of OPEC donors as a group remained substantially higher than the average of ODA by DAC countries over the same period by a margin of almost 10:1. The absolute amounts of assistance, of course, are substantially lower than those provided by DAC countries.

Table 2 Concessional financial outflows as a share of gross national production (GNP): disbursements (per cent)

	1977	1978	1979	1980
Algeria	0.54	0.88	0.90	0.87
Iran	0.29	0.37	0.03	0.00
Iraq	1.19	2.50	3.38	3.21
Kuwait	10.62	9.43	4.12	4.61
Libyan Arab Jamahariya	0.69	0.92	0.61	0.88
Qatar	8.01	6.10	6.66	5.81
Saudi Arabia	4.81	3.81	3.92	3.15
United Arab Emirates	10.32	6.40	6.10	4.70
Venezuela	2.03	1.83	1.09	1.21

Source: UNCTAD (see Table 1).

11. The following further conclusions may be drawn from an analysis of the nine countries' financial assistance to developing countries during the 1977–80 period:

(a) As is shown in Table 3, the major recipients of concessional assistance from OPEC donors as a group over the period 1977–80 have been the 'most seriously affected' countries, which received US $8,957.6 million, followed by the 'least developed countries', which received US $5,302.9 million, and the land-locked countries—US $384.79 million. It should be noted that some developing countries are members of more than one group, which means that these percentages are not additive.

Table 3 All OPEC donors Concessional Assistance: amounts received by recipient groups (US $ million)

	1977	1978	1979	1980
Land-locked countries	144.89	70.08	63.58	106.24
Least-developed countries	1,441.27	1,093.27	762.98	2,005.43
MSA	3,530.74	2,060.41	1,307.98	2,058.55
	Shares as percentage			
	1977	1978	1979	1980
Land-locked countries	1.9	1.0	0.7	0.8
Least-developed countries	18.9	15.6	8.4	15.1
MSA	46.3	29.4	14.4	15.5

Source: UNCTAD (see Table 1).

(b) An increased reliance is observed on the national and multilateral institutions for channelling financial resources and co-financing projects in developing countries.

(c) Institutions of OPEC countries have, in the past few years, made major advances on the organization and techniques of development assistance, including the adoption of standardized documentation and procedures for project appraisal, loan agreements, procurements, disbursement and the use of joint operational missions and the interchange of appraisal and supervision reports. Co-financing *among these institutions* has covered 60 per cent of total lending in 1980 as against 25 per cent in 1977. In the administration of a co-financed loan the participating institutions tend to delegate the responsibility of administration of the loan to only one of them.

Multilateral Institutions

12. Since the early 1970s, the new multilateral institutions backed by OPEC countries have played an important role in channelling flows of financial resources to developing countries, particularly in Africa and Asia. Assistance given by these

institutions has largely been in the form of concessional loan finance for development projects. In addition, other forms of assistance have been provided by some of the institutions. The OPEC Fund combines balance of payment support with lending programmes, as well as channelling assistance to other development agencies. The Islamic Development Bank engages in certain forms of export credit. The Arab Fund for Economic and Social Development provides certain types of technical assistance. It also continues to act as the technical secretariat for co-ordination among Arab national development finance institutions and OPEC multilateral institutions on whose behalf it issues quarterly reports covering loans and technical assistance provided by these institutions.

13. As shown in Table 4, the total value of commitments granted by the OPEC multilateral institutions over the period 1977–80 amounted to US $2,012.6 million, representing over 56 per cent of their combined paid-in capital. This ratio of commitments to paid-in capital demonstrates the rapidity with which the OPEC multilateral institutions have been transferring resources to other developing countries. These institutions have committed financial assistance averaging more than US $503 million a year.

14. Recent operations by OPEC multilateral institutions show a marked emphasis on infrastructure. The share of this sector represented almost 26 per cent of total commitments by the four institutions over the period 1977–80. The development of infrastructure, broadly defined as the construction of road networks, installation or improvements of telecommunications, water-works and irrigation schemes, benefits more than one sector and in many instances it is a prerequisite for the development of agriculture and rural development, the promotion of industry and the expansion of trade (see Table 5).

15. Industry and mining remain the second highest sector with about 17 per cent of total commitments. Although assistance to this sector has been mainly allocated to large projects, small-scale industries have by no means been neglected. For efficiency and administrative convenience, assistance to such industries has taken the form of lines of credit to national banks or

Table 4 Concessional financial flows from OPEC multilateral funds (1977–80) (US $ million)

	Commitments				Disbursements			
	1977	1978	1979	1980	1977	1978	1979	1980
OPEC Fund	251.2	152.8	212.9	259.1	160.8	82.8	83.3	157.6
ISDB	65.4	141.1	76.2	73.1	1.2	31.3	72.3	102.4
AFESD	360.0	–	95.0	92.0	56.9	189.4	124.9	95.0
BADEA	66.3	72.3	49.1	46.1	18.2	51.3	37.8	39.4
Total	742.9	366.2	433.2	470.3	237.1	354.8	318.3	394.4

Source: UNCTAD (see Table 1).

Table 5 Concessional financial flows from OPEC multilateral funds (1977–80): commitments (US $ million)

	Infra-structure	Industry and mining	Agriculture and fisheries	Primary energy	Technical assistance	Education	Balance of payments support	Others	Total
OPEC Fund	191.5	81.6	21.5	197.2	28.5	–	371.9	–	892.2
ISDB	244.7	230.7	61.6	–	8.6	–	999.0	–	1,544.6
AFESD	245.0	92.0	75.5	136.6	9.5	–	–	–	558.6
BADEA	107.8	77.2	21.0	28.2	1.2	–	–	0.5	235.9
Total	789.0	481.5	179.6	362.0	47.8	–	1,370.9	0.5	3,231.3
	(Percentage)								
OPEC Fund	21.5	9.1	2.4	22.1	3.2	–	41.7	–	100
ISDB	15.8	14.9	4.0	–	0.6	–	64.7	–	100
AFESD	43.9	16.5	13.5	24.4	1.7	–	–	–	100
BADEA	45.7	32.7	8.9	12.0	0.5	–	–	0.2	100

Source: UNCTAD (see Table 1).

financial organizations. Because of their experience and knowledge of investment opportunities, local financial institutions are thought to be better suited to undertake the channelling of these funds to small industries.

16. The energy sector, which ranks third in importance, accounted for 10.8 per cent of total cumulative assistance. Most of the four institutions under review have made indications that more assistance in the future will be allocated to energy-related projects. Involvement in the exploration of the energy potential, including hydro-electric power, is likely to be stepped up.

17. Agriculture has received less attention, a tendency which is likely to persist for some time. One reason for this pattern of assistance relates to the fact that modernization of agriculture and rural areas in general is more prone to obstacles than that of other sectors.

18. The relatively high figure for balance of payments support (US $1,371 million in 1977–80) includes OPEC Fund lending for this purpose, plus the Islamic Development Bank financing of foreign trade.

19. With a 70 per cent overall grant element, the OPEC multilateral institutions remain among the cheapest source of finance available to developing countries. The ISDB, for example, charges no interest on its loans with long maturities and offers a grace period of between three and a half and six years. The other OPEC multilateral institutions have similarly highly concessional assistance. The bulk of multilateral assistance has been channelled to the 'most seriously affected countries', which accounted for over 72 per cent, while the land-locked and least developed countries received 22 per cent and 41 per cent respectively.

National Institutions

20. Prior to 1973, only two OPEC members, Kuwait and the United Arab Emirates, possessed national institutions for channelling resources to other developing countries. The Kuwait Fund for Arab Economic Development, established in 1961, is

Table 6 Concessional financial flows from Arab national funds (1977–80) (US $ million)

	Commitments				Disbursements			
	1977	1978	1979	1980	1977	1978	1979	1980
Kuwait fund	397.1	209.2	363.3	266.4	190.9	197.5	223.9	316.3
Saudi fund	771.5	620.1	463.5	596.0	153.7	217.4	357.1	368.4
Abu Dhabi fund	137.6	45.3	104.6	98.5	92.3	43.2	79.3	113.2
Iraq fund	55.0	79.5	106.3	253.4	–	–	–	–
Total	1,361.2	954.1	1,037.7	1,214.3	436.9	458.1	660.3	797.9

Source: UNCTAD (see Table 1).

Table 7 Sectoral distribution of financial assistance from Arab National Funds, commitments (1977–80) (US $ million)

	Infra-structure	Industry and mining	Agriculture and fisheries	Primary energy	Technical assistance	Education	Balance of payments support	Others	Total
Kuwait fund	577.9	325.8	49.2	344.2	3.2	–	–	–	1,300.3
Saudi fund	1,295.1	115.7	271.1	717.2	–	61.8	–	–	2,460.9
Abu Dhabi fund	146.0	320.5	45.3	42.1	3.3	–	–	–	557.2
Iraq fund	165.2	102.3	87.4	92.3	–	–	89.6	–	536.8
Total	2,184.2	864.3	453.0	1,195.8	6.5	61.8	89.6	–	4,855.2
	(Percentage)								
Kuwait fund	44.4	25.1	3.8	26.5	0.2	–	–	–	100.0
Saudi fund	52.6	4.7	11.0	29.2	–	2.5	–	–	100.0
Abu Dhabi fund	26.2	57.5	8.1	7.6	0.6	–	–	–	100.0
Iraq fund	30.8	19.0	16.3	17.2	–	–	16.7	–	100.0

Source: UNCTAD (see Table 1).

not only the oldest OPEC development institution, but also has the largest capital. The United Arab Emirates established its fund (ADFAED) in 1971, which has since risen to prominence among Arab financial institutions. While both these institutions had initially been established to assist in the development of Arab countries, a change in their statutes took place after 1974 to enable them to lend to non-Arab developing countries.

21. The recently established Saudi Fund for Development and the Iraqi Fund for External Development have been very active since their inception and have no geographic limitations on their lending operations.

22. As shown in Table 6, total cumulative concessional commitments by all Arab National Funds over the 1977–80 period amounted to US $4,567.3 million* of which over US $2,800 million, or 61 per cent of total commitments, have already been disbursed.

23. The relative contributions by the four institutions of total loan commitments over the 1977–80 period were as follows: US $2,461 million or 50.7 per cent by the Saudi Fund; US $1,300 million or 26.8 per cent by the Kuwait Fund; US $557 million or 11.5 per cent by the Abu Dhabi Fund; and US $537 million or 11 per cent by the Iraqi Fund.

24. The bulk of concessional assistance provided by Arab national funds is directed to the financing of development projects. With the exception of some highly concessional loans provided by the Iraqi Fund in support of the importation of Iraqi oil, the Arab national funds do not normally engage in foreign trade financing or balance of payments support. Excluding the Iraqi loans that were extended for this latter purpose, the sectoral allocation of project financing of the four institutions was as follows: US $2,184.2 million or 45 per cent for projects in infrastructure; US $1,195.8 million or 24.6 per cent for projects in energy; US $864.3 million or 17.8 per cent for projects in industry and mining; and US $453 million or 10.3 per cent for projects in agriculture (see Table 7).

* The total in Table 5 differs from that in Table 4 because the latter includes both concessional and non-concessional assistance.

APPENDIX I

Report by the Rapporteur Général on the Jamaica Meeting on ECDC finance

Part I

1. Pursuant to the decision adopted at the Caracas High Level Conference on Economic Co-operation Among Developing Countries, there was convened in Kingston, Jamaica, from 26 to 31 March 1982 the Meeting of Experts of the Group of 77 on ECDC Finance.

2. Representatives of the following countries participated in the discussions:

Algeria	Iraq	Peru
Argentina	Jamaica	Philippines
Bangladesh	Republic of Korea	Romania
Brazil	Democratic People's Republic of Korea	Saudi Arabia
Cuba		Somalia
Ecuador	Kuwait	Sri Lanka
Egypt	Malaysia	Suriname
Gabon	Malta	Tanzania
Ghana	Mexico	Trinidad and Tobago
Guyana	Morocco	Tunisia
Haiti	Nigeria	Uganda
India	Pakistan	Venezuela
Indonesia		

3. The terms of reference of the Meeting were:

(a) the examination, in the context of paragraph 79 of the feasibility of a financing facility to meet the balance of payments problems of developing countries with contributions from interested developing countries and administered by them;

(paragraph 66B of the Caracas decisions) and

(b) to examine the proposals made by the Non-Aligned Movement and The Group of 77, and to propose concrete measures by the end of 1981 for financial cooperation in the field of development financing, *inter alia*, the entry into force of the Non-Aligned Solidarity Fund, and the bank for developing countries as indicated by the Group of 77 Ministerial Meeting at Arusha in 1979

(paragraph 79 of the Caracas decisions).

4. The Meeting was opened by the Right Honourable Edward Seaga, Prime Minister of Jamaica.

5. At its first plenary session, the Meeting unanimously elected its Chairman, H.E. Sir E. Richardson (Jamaica) and its Bureau, composed of the following persons:

Vice Chairman:	Mr M. Besse Khouad	(Algeria)
	Mr L. H. Periera de Fonseca	(Brazil)
	H.E. A. Mongongo-Nzabi	(Gabon)
	Mr A. Al-Ebrahim	(Kuwait)
	Ms R. Lajous de Solana	(Mexico)
	Mr O. Esan	(Nigeria)
	H.E. R. O. Arcilla	(Philippines)
	H.E. M. Charara	(Saudi Arabia)
	Ms T. Urdaneta	(Venezuela)
Rapporteur Général:	H.E. Dr. Lal Jayawardena	(Sri Lanka)

6. The Meeting also agreed that the record of its deliberations would be made available in the form of the present Report by the Rapporteur Général. The broad issues central to financial co-operation among developing countries were presented to the Meeting at its first plenary session by Mr D. Avramovic, Director of the support staff which has prepared the documents presented to the Meeting. (The Agenda and a list of these documents are appended on pp. 201–2.) Mr Avramovic emphasized that the underlying principle of the approach taken to ECDC financing was that of joint and mutual interest among developing countries. This principle seemed to emerge from the Caracas document and spokesmen of both the surplus and the deficit

developing countries had announced it on several occasions. For the surplus countries, the main economic interest in co-operation derived from the desire to diversify their assets, secure additional sources of supply, and moderate the increase in import prices through suitable productive investments. Hence they were especially interested in promoting direct investment and joint ventures in the deficit developing countries. Most oil-exporting countries were also anxious to obtain modern technology and develop domestic skills, and counted on their technologically more advanced developing countries to help them in this process, for example, through joint ventures located in the oil-exporting countries, Finally, it was worth noting that the returns to capital in the developing economies would probably be higher, and their markets for petroleum and other goods would be growing faster, than was the case in the industrialized countries.

7. Mr Avramovic reminded the meeting that for the deficit countries the most urgent need was for balance of payments assistance to help them adjust to the enormous deterioration in the terms of exchange they had experienced in recent years: their import prices had risen sharply, the cost of capital had undergone a major upward shift, while their export commodity prices had now fallen to their lowest levels in real terms in the past thirty-five years. These countries were also interested in joint ventures with, and direct investment by, the surplus countries; furthermore, they needed organized assistance for the development of their energy and other mineral resources; finally, they needed support for the expansion of exports which was almost their only salvation over the medium and long run.

8. The existing aid institutions were likely to continue to be the main vehicles through which concessional assistance would be channelled to the less fortunate parts of the developing world, and that, conversely, new institutional mechanisms which might develop would have to be such as to be able to mobilize large funds on a continuing basis from the capital markets and other sources. Furthermore, the funds provided by a new institution could not be expected to substitute for the commitments of the developed countries. However, the new institution might

provide resources, or help mobilize such resources, for some of the strategic areas which had been deprived of funds, but which were of critical importance for the improvement of the position of the developing countries in the world economy, while at the same time providing reasonable financial returns and security.

9. These areas were the gaps in the financing structure which had been identified in the agenda for the meeting: joint ventures, energy investment, export credit finance, commodity finance, regional reserve arrangements and perhaps special payments arrangements for key imports. An institution which could handle joint investments and some of the other gaps discussed could also perform the functions of a merchant banking facility. It would then have the advantage of participating directly in international capital markets and could both create new sources of capital and develop the capacity to provide continuing and solid financial and management advice.

10. Mr Avramovic argued that, in order to handle simultaneously both the development finance and balance of payments financing matters, what might be needed was a South Bank Group, in which the OPEC Fund would continue as a major soft concessional lending agency, with its own capital structure; while the rest would be accommodated by a new agency—a Bank for Developing Countries—and would stand parallel. Such a new institution would be expected to work in close co-operation with the existing financing agencies, both regional and interregional and would also work closely with banks and producing and marketing firms in the developed as well as the developing countries.

11. For such an institution to become a reality, major financial support would be needed from the surplus countries, but also a substantial equity stake would need to be forthcoming from the deficit countries. Also needed would be a co-ordinating forum of developing countries which would include the interested countries and agencies and provide an organized framework for discussion of joint approaches on issues of monetary and financial co-operation.

In preparing the documentation, the staff had refrained from spelling out the details of a possible capital structure, operating principles, profitability conditions, borrowing capability and decision-making structure of a Bank for Developing Countries. It was believed that the first job to be done at the Meeting was to examine the strength of the case for establishing such an institution and to agree on some key guiding principles. If the Expert Group concluded that the case existed and agreed on the basic principles, the next job would be to prepare a specific project proposal for such a Bank.

12. Mr A. McIntyre, Deputy Secretary General of UNCTAD, expressed on behalf of the Secretary General, Mr G. Corea, UNCTAD's deep and continuing support for ECDC activities. He pledged UNCTAD's co-operation within the limits of its financial resources and its existing commitments to promote effective support for the follow-up work.

13. Mr W. Mashler, Senior Director of the Division for Global and International Projects of the UNDP, indicated that the UNDP would be prepared to continue its support for ECDC with particular reference to financial co-operation among developing countries. UNDP, together with UNCTAD, had provided support for the work preparatory to this meeting. For the follow-up, UNDP would make available up to $350,000 to continue to finance the work co-ordinated by Mr Avramovic in preparation for the Group of Experts meeting in Jamaica as part of the ECDC programme, for a further period of two years in the context of joint ECDC activities with UNCTAD. An amount of approximately $35,000–$40,000 remained from the contribution for the preparatory work and this was available for the follow-up. However, he indicated that the programme would require substantially larger sums and the Group of 77 will need to consider at an early stage how it could make a financial contribution to complement UNDP's assistance in this area.

14. The discussions in the meeting were based upon a shared perception of the existence of significant mutual interests among developing countries in strengthening collective self-reliance by promoting economically viable development projects and programmes in different areas. This was an integral part of the collective action among the developing countries for

the restructuring of international economic relations, and should in no way be construed as derogating from the historical responsibility of the developed countries to co-operate in implementing the goals, targets, and objectives agreed by the international community. The need for special effort to alleviate the problems of least developed countries was stressed.

A. Development projects, joint ventures and export credits

15. It was agreed that economically viable development projects would be capable of being financed by loans on market-related terms. Projects so financed would, generally speaking, complement developing countries' joint venture investment projects, based partly on equity and partly on loan financing. Joint ventures should specifically emphasize and exploit to the largest extent possible the comparative economic advantage of developing countries, in order to ensure the optional use of available resources, including raw materials, capital, technological and managerial expertise, supply of skills, and transfer of technology. Each country's policies regarding foreign investment should be respected.

16. It was accepted that host developing countries wishing to attract joint-venture investment would need to develop the necessary domestic legislative and incentive framework. The Meeting recognized that progress was already being made by developing countries in attracting investments from other developing countries and it was suggested that this experience with joint ventures should be reviewed through country studies. Further, the Meeting accepted that this progress could be accelerated through deliberate and suitable policy action.

17. Doing so would also require co-ordinated action in investment promotion including:

(a) the exchange of information on existing joint ventures, markets, and legal and incentive structures affecting investments;
(b) pre-project technical assistance and project identification, appraisal and development; and
(c) brokerage facilities to bring together potential investors and

other sources of funds such as commercial and investment banks.

18. It was agreed that a significant gap existed in the area of export credit finance, especially in some regions. Its treatment would require provision of adequate finance for export credits and of guarantees for such credits and this could also be done in the context of joint ventures.

B. Energy investment

19. The Meeting expressed its appreciation of the final outcome of the discussion at the Meeting of Inter-Governmental Experts held in Baghdad, 1–4 March 1982, on the Iraqi proposal for the establishment of a World Fund. The Meeting agreed that the Group of 77 should continue its effort to establish the World Bank energy affiliate with a view to financing both public and private projects. Complementary arrangements for insuring against the risks of oil exploration should be introduced by interested countries. This would facilitate the 'energy transition'. In so far as projects for energy development proper proved to be economically viable, they would also benefit from whatever institutional arrangements might be set up for promoting developing countries' joint-venture investment projects. All arrangements affecting energy should be consistent with the principle of the permanent sovereignty of countries over their natural resources.

C. Balance of payments

20. The Meeting agreed that the traditional distinction between development finance and balance of payments support had diminishing relevance for developing countries given the structural nature of their balance of payments problems. It was suggested that direct balance of payments support should form an important part of South–South economic co-operation. The efforts through existing South–South institutions should be more effecitvely co-ordinated. Further thought would need to be given to the modalities of such co-ordination.

21. The Meeting discussed commodity finance, pointing to the

fact that an increased real return on exports of developing countries would automatically lead to an improvement in their balance of payments. Further elaboration of measures for improving commodity prices would need to take account of ongoing work on stabilization measures as proposed by Madagascar and entailed in the UNCTAD Integrated Programme for Commodities. In this regard, the Meeting felt that every effort should be made to ensure the early entry into force of the Common Fund. Regional and subregional measures taken in a South-South context should not impede the process of ratification of the Fund, and should avoid the duplication of tasks.

22. The Meeting considered other balance of payments measures, particularly regional credit arrangements and steps to remedy adverse movements in the balance of payments arising from deterioration in the terms of trade. Some examples of regional balance of payments support mechanisms were mentioned, e.g. in Latin America, and it was felt that existing mechanisms should be linked on the basis of mutual interests. A need was expressed for similar mechanisms in other regions. It was agreed that the treatment of this problem should not focus exclusively on imports of a single commodity no matter how important. Possible solutions should also be linked to the effective promotion of development projects and joint ventures.

D. Institutional issues

23. The Meeting considered whether these functions should best be left to be discharged by the evolution of existing processes and institutional arrangements or whether they should also be included or grouped within the functions of a new Southern institution—the Bank for Developing Countries. In this context, the Meeting also examined the Non-Aligned Solidarity Fund which had been open for signature since 1975, and noted that there were few signatures and fewer ratifications. The Meeting was unable to reach firm conclusions regarding the technical aspects relating to its entry into force. It was, however, agreed that steps should be taken to make the Fund operational as soon as possible and that any examination of the possible establishment of new institutions should take into account the reasons for the failure to ratify the Fund.

24. There was considerable support for the view that a Bank for Developing Countries directed towards promoting economically viable development projects and programmes in different areas and for balance of payments support was needed to supplement resources from traditional international finance institutions given their present inflexibility and constraints. Such an institution would play a catalytic role in promoting co-ordinated investment programmes involving joint ventures consistent with the national legislation of interested countries, complemented by strengthened export credit facilities. Such an institution could also promote the favourable investment climates needed for joint ventures.

25. In the absence of a Bank for Developing Countries, a heavy burden would be cast on existing financial mechanisms and a number of gaps in the structure of development financing of vital concern to the developing countries would remain unfilled.

26. The Meeting agreed that a technical study would be required of the scale and characteristics of the Bank for Developing Countries, covering both development and balance of payments measures as discussed above. The meeting noted that the study should avoid emphasizing the role of one particular group of countries within the South as the sole vehicle for financial co-operation within the South as this would create avoidable schisms within the South and would be tantamount to assigning to this group of countries the role that should be assumed by the North. Further, the study should proceed on the basis that participation in the Bank would be of a voluntary character, involving interested countries.

27. The Meeting also took note of a number of technical matters which the study should take account of. These concerned the following:

(a) projections of cash flows and the volume of resources required including callable capital to cope respectively with project financing and balance of payments support requirements of developing countries;
(b) the illustrative financing schedule that would build up to the required amount step by step;

(c) how far the institution would secure 'additional' resources in relation to amounts mobilized through existing institutions;
(d) how to distribute the paid-in and callable capital obligations as between developing countries differently situated in respect of financial strength, bearing in mind that many inconvertible currencies may be involved;
(e) the possibility of relying upon the intermediation of an agent bank instead of a new institution to discharge the functions required;
(f) the implications under the Caracas Programme of Action of any financial graduation for countries that have a relatively larger GNP per capita;
(g) ways of securing better co-operation between the Group of 24 and the arrangements for financial co-operation within the ECDC.

28. This would enable the Group of 77 at a subsequent meeting to take the appropriate political decisions within the context of the Caracas Programme of Action. The Meeting adopted an outline of a technical study on the feasibility of establishing a Bank for Developing Countries and establishing guidelines for the scope of this study and for the organization of further work in follow-up to the Meeting; these decisions are contained in Part II of the Report. The Meeting took note of Part I of the Report.

29. The representative of Algeria, speaking on behalf of the Group of 77, expressed their appreciation to the Right Honourable Edward Seaga, Prime Minister of Jamaica, for the close attention he had given to the Meeting and for the inspiring address he made at the opening session. On behalf of the delegations attending the Meeting, he expressed thanks and appreciation to the Government and people of Jamaica for their hospitality and the excellent organization of the Meeting. A special note of appreciation was also conveyed to the Chairman for his efficient organization of the Meeting which had helped significantly in reaching the important agreements which were adopted.

30. The Honourable Basil Buck, M.P., Minister of State in the

Office of the Prime Minister and leader of the Jamaican delegation, thanked the delegations for their kind words and conveyed his expressions of gratitude to all those who had contributed in making the Meeting such a constructive one. In particular, he expressed his appreciation for the detailed preparatory work undertaken by Mr Avramovic and the staff of UNCTAD which allowed the delegates an opportunity for a useful exchange of views. The Meeting had ended on a positive note and further work could now be continued on this basis.

Part II

Follow-up to Jamaica Meeting: outline of technical study of the feasibility of a 'Bank for Developing Countries'

1. Terms of reference.
   (a) Paragraph 66B) of the Caracas Programme of Action
   (b) Paragraph 79)

2. Guidelines for the Scope of Study emerging from the Group of Experts meeting in Jamaica.

3. Proposals for a 'Bank for Developing Countries' and its possible scope.

4. A. *Functions*
   1. Development projects, joint ventures, including export credit.
   2. (1) + balance of payments support.

   B. Capital structure and borrowing powers for each of the functions as listed under (A) above.

   C. Capital subscriptions and payments and decision-making structure.

4. Separate institutional entities/windows grouped as appropriate, including commodity finance and support for regional credit arrangements.

5. Conclusions and recommendations.

Guidelines for the Scope of Study

The Meeting agreed that the technical study should be based on a realistic assessment of the current economic situation and of the long-term development perspectives of developing countries and should reflect the following:

(1) requirements of development finance and balance of payments support;
(2) financial viability should be assured as well as access to international capital markets;
(3) participation in the Bank would be based on the principle of collective and equitable sharing of obligations by all interested members of G.77 as well as on the basis of joint and mutual benefits;
(4) in order to avoid duplication of tasks in the operations of the Bank, it should ensure adequate co-ordination with existing subregional, regional and international financial institutions.

This strengthened co-operation among developing countries would not relieve the developed countries of their responsibilities for supporting the development objectives of developing countries.

The study should take account of other existing proposals of a similar nature, e.g. Iraqi proposal for a World Fund and the proposed IBID of UNIDO.

Organization of work

1. The Meeting agreed that the Government of Jamaica (as host of the Group of Experts meeting), with the co-operation and participation of other interested governments of the Group of 77, should co-ordinate the preparation of the technical study, and requested the UNDP and UNCTAD to continue to give their full support to the project, as part of the programme of ECDC.

2. The first draft of the technical study should be circulated through the G.77 in New York to member governments as soon as it is available.

3. The Chairman of the Group of Experts of the Jamaica Meeting

will consult with the Chairman of the G.77 in New York, the Government of the Philippines (as host of the meeting of the Inter-governmental Follow-up and Co-ordination Committee on ECDC) and interested governments, with a view to determining the appropriate timing for further work at the intergovernmental level.

Documentation for the Jamaica Meeting

Title	*Symbol*
Provisional Agenda	
The Jamaica Meeting on Finance: Major Questions	Finance: 1
Joint Ventures among Developing Countries	Finance: 2
Energy Investment	Finance: 3
Export Credit	Finance: 4
Commodity Finance	Finance: 5
The Financing of Regional Credit Arrangements among Developing Countries	Finance: 6
Payments Arrangements for Oil Imports	Finance: 7
The Caracas Programme on Finance: Substance and Implementation	Finance: 8
The Non-Aligned Movement and the Group of 77: a Case Study of the Non-Aligned Solidarity Fund for Economic and Social Development and a Survey of Monetary and Financial Co-operation among Developing Countries	Finance: 9
Review of Proposals for Third World Financing Co-operation	Finance: 10
Promotion of Investment Flows among Developing Countries: a Possible Multilateral Investment Guarantee Scheme	Finance: 11
Concessional Development Assistance by OPEC Members and Institutions to other Developing Countries	Finance: 12
Report of the High-Level Consultations Meeting on Financial Co-operation among Developing Countries	Finance: 14

Group of 77 ECDC Meeting on Financial Co-operation Provisional Agenda

1. Opening of Meeting
2. Opening of address by the Honourable Prime Minister of Jamaica
3. Adoption of the Agenda and organization of work
4. Election of Officers
5. Statement of Chairman
6. Development Finance:
   (i) Joint Ventures
   (ii) Export Credit
   (iii) Energy
7. Balance-of-Payments Support:
   (i) Commodity Finance
   (ii) Special Import Payment Arrangements
   (iii) Assistance to Regional and Subregional Reserves Schemes
8. Institutional Framework including:
   (i) The Non-Aligned Solidarity Fund
   (ii) The Bank for Developing Countries (South Bank)
9. Follow-up on Group of Experts Meeting held in Kingston
10. Closure of meeting.

APPENDIX II*

V. Finance

58. A. The Committee considered the *Report of the Meeting of Experts of the Group of 77 on Finance and Balance of Payments* (Doc.IFCC.1/G.77/B–8), held in Baghdad, 1–4 March 1982, concerning the proposal to establish a World Fund as the mechanism to alleviate the financial burdens imposed on the developing countries due to the inflation imported from developed countries and adjustments in oil prices. The report was introduced by the delegation of Iraq.

59. The Committee agreed that the issue on the establishment of a World Fund is crucial. However, the Committee raised certain points regarding the procedure of implementing the proposal and the technical requirements involved.

60. Some delegations expressed the view that the proposal could be endorsed by the Meeting and submitted to the Ministers of the Group of 77 at their meeting in September 1982 during which the contents of the proposal could be analysed further. Thereafter, it could be left to the Ministers to decide on the next appropriate action to take, such as the timing of consultation with the developed countries if it is deemed appropriate or looking into the possibility of convening an experts' meeting. A few delegations considered that a decision could not be taken prior to having the support of the developed countries to the proposal. A few delegations also pointed out that the Fund might be a duplication of existing financial institutions and might represent a risk of proliferation of the same.

*This is an extract from Doc. IFCC.I/G.77/Rpt.1: 'Manila Follow-Up Action Adopted by the First Meeting of the Intergovernmental Follow-Up and Co-ordination Committee on Economic Co-operation Among Developing Countries', Manila, 23–8 August 1982.

61. The Committee noted with appreciation the recommendations of the experts' group meeting in Baghdad and agreed to submit the proposal to the Ministers' Meeting of the Group of 77 in New York for further consideration.

62. B. The Committee also considered the *Report of the Rapporteur Général on the Jamaica Meeting on ECDC Finance* (Doc.IFCC.1/G.77/B–9), held on 26–31 March 1982 in Kingston, Jamaica, pursuant to the decision adopted at the Caracas High-Level Conference on Economic Co-operation Among Developing Countries, and within the context of the terms of reference as contained in paragraphs 66B and 79 of the Caracas decision.

63. The Report of the Rapporteur Général on the Kingston Meeting on ECDC Finance was introduced by the delegation of Jamaica which also informed the meeting of the progress made with respect to the preparation of a technical study on the feasibility of a bank for developing countries.

64. Many delegations expressed the view that the establishment of a South–South Bank was important.

65. During the discussion, distinction was made between Part I and Part II of the Report as different views were expressed on the results of the Kingston Meeting.

66. In this regard, many delegations suggested that the Committee should only take note of Part I, while others were of the view that Part II, which contains the outline of the feasibility study, should be approved and endorsed by the Committee and submitted to the Ministers of the G.77. On the other hand, some delegations felt strongly that the outline was limited in scope. Nevertheless, it was agreed that the outline could serve as a general framework for the feasibilty study. It was stressed strongly that there is a need for the active participation of the developing countries' experts in the preparation of the study.

Actions taken by the Committee

65. The Committee took note of the Rapporteur Général's Report of the meeting on ECDC Finance held in Jamaica, 26–31 March 1982, and recommended to the Ministerial Meeting of the Group of 77 to be held in September 1982 that a technical study on the feasibility of the Bank for Developing Countries be undertaken on the basis of Part II of the Report as a general framework, without prejudice to the range of the functions to be covered by the proposed bank.

66. The Committee agreed to request the Secretary-General of UNCTAD, in close co-operation with interested financial institutions of the developing countries, to give all necessary assistance to facilitate the completion of the study by preparing the appropriate technical documentation. The study will be prepared by a Group of Governmental Experts of the Group of 77.

67. The study should be submitted through the Chairman of the Group of 77 in New York to the IFCC in its 1983 meeting.

68. *G–24 Report on ECDC*
The Committee took note of the section dealing with ECDC in the report of the Twenty-Fourth Meeting of the Finance Ministers of the Intergovernmental Group of 24 on International Monetary Issues held in Helsinki on 11 May 1982 (Doc.IFCC.1/G.77/B–13).

Matters taken by the Committee

[illegible]

[illegible] agreed [illegible] to the [illegible]

[illegible]

[illegible]